MUSCLE CARS
IN DETAIL   No. 4

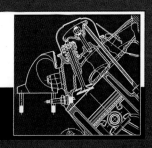

1969 *Chevrolet*
CAMARO
SS

Bobby Kimbrough

D1557954

CarTech®

CarTech®

CarTech®, Inc.
838 Lake Street South
Forest Lake, MN 55025
Phone: 651-277-1200 or 800-551-4754
Fax: 651-277-1203
www.cartechbooks.com

Edit by Paul Johnson
Layout by Monica Seiberlich

ISBN 978-1-61325-274-1
Item No. CT564

Library of Congress Cataloging-in-Publication Data Available

Written, edited, and designed in the U.S.A.
Printed in China
10 9 8 7 6 5 4 3 2 1

Front Cover:
Chevrolet's L89-equipped Camaro SS was the most powerful factory build.

Title Page:
The L78 and L88 big-blocks are considered high-performance 396 SS engines. Virtually identical, except for the Winters aluminum cylinder heads on the L88 version, these were conservatively rated at 375 hp.

Contents Page:
The Z11 Indy Pace Car Edition convertible is a great piece of Camaro and Indianapolis 500 history. Returning as the pace car after holding that honor in 1967, the Camaro SS, featuring the white with Hugger Orange stripes, is one of the most popular Indy pace cars of all time.

DISTRIBUTION BY:

Europe
PGUK
63 Hatton Garden
London EC1N 8LE, England
Phone: 020 7061 1980 • Fax: 020 7242 3725
www.pguk.co.uk

Australia
Renniks Publications Ltd.
3/37-39 Green Street
Banksmeadow, NSW 2109, Australia
Phone: 2 9695 7055 • Fax: 2 9695 7355
www.renniks.com

■ INTRODUCTION 4

■ CHAPTER 1: Advent of the Camaro SS ... 7

History of the Super Sport.................................... 7
Major Changes in 1969 11
Vehicle Identification 12
GM Part Numbering System 12
VIN Decoding 13
Trim Plates 14
The Five Camaro Models of 1969 14
Rally Sport Package 17

■ CHAPTER 2: Camaro SS
    and Special Edition Cars 19

Camaro Super Sport... 20
Indianapolis 500 Pace Car and Pace Car Replica.......... 21
The Official Pace Cars 23
Race Winner Replica.. 24
Festival Cars 27
Z11 Pace Car Replicas 27
Z10 Pace Car 32
Dealer-Modified Camaro SS Models.................. 33

■ CHAPTER 3: Engine Options 36

Small-Block Engines 37
Chevy 350-ci Small-Block SS Engine Options 39
L48 350-ci 295-hp... 39
Big-Block Engines... 41
L35 396-ci 325-hp and L34 396-ci 350-hp 43
L78 396-ci 375-hp and L89 396-ci 375-hp 45
L89 Aluminum Cylinder Heads........................... 47
Distributors 48
Carburetors.. 51

■ CHAPTER 4: Drivetrain and Chassis ... 52

Manual Transmissions.. 53
Automatic Transmissions 55
Shifters.. 56
Driveshaft 58
Rear Axle 59
Coil and Leaf Springs 62
Brakes.. 63

■ CHAPTER 5: Interior 66

Standard Interior... 67
Seat Belts... 71
Custom Interior... 74
Special Interior... 74
Other Interior Options with Special RPO Packages 75
Gauges and Monitoring Systems 75
Speedometers 77
Other Instruments 77
Features and Individual Options 78
Radios.. 80
Interior Summary 81

■ CHAPTER 6: Exterior 82

Paint.. 82
Glass.. 83
Lamps and Markers 85
Standard Base Camaro Exterior 85
Rally Sport Exterior 86
Camaro Super Sport Exterior 86
Camaro SS/RS Exterior 87
Vinyl and Convertible Tops................................ 87
Spoiler Option 88
Grille... 89
Emblems and Badging 89
Striping 92
Wheels and Tires 93

INTRODUCTION

While the Camaro was under development, it was known internally as the Panther. Sources in General Motors have claim that as many as 2,000 names were considered before settling on the Camaro name. Of the first-generation Camaro models, muscle car enthusiasts consider the 1969 models the most desirable.

Although it may have been rushed to the market at the outset, few automobiles left a mark on history as did the 1969 Chevrolet Camaro. Officials at General Motors declared several times that the iconic Camaro was initially rushed to market in 1967 to compete with the Ford Mustang. "The Camaro should not have been a design success," said Ed Welburn, GM's vice president of global design, "as it was based on existing architecture and admittedly hurried to market to address the personal coupe revolution occurring with the baby boomer customers."

Welburn's comments came in the form of a GM press release during the Camaro's 2009 re-launch. "The 1969 model is the iconic Camaro to me," Welburn added, "From the dual-plane grille design and speed lines stamped into the fenders and doors, it was original and distinctive."

Before the fifth-generation Camaros were re-introduced after an eight-year hiatus, General Motors began releasing reviews from its engineering and design crews discussing the early-model Camaros, paying close attention to the 1969. "It is one of the most popular and sought

1969 Chevrolet Camaro SS
In Detail No. 4

after Camaros of all time," GM Heritage Center manager Greg Wallace said. "Like the 1957 Chevy, this Camaro will go down as a styling highpoint for General Motors and Chevrolet." To no one's surprise, the 2010 Camaro was released heavily loaded with those 1969 styling cues. Wallace confirmed the observation by saying, "When you look at the generation-five Camaro concept car, there's no secret that it looks like the 1969 Camaro."

When the 1969 Camaro was originally offered, it was met with great public adoration of its timeless rounded body design, sharp waist, and simplistic form that was lower and wider than previous models. Performance enthusiasts were infatuated with the engine options while the rest of the car buying public lusted for the sporty design and feel of Chevrolet's contribution to the pony car wars.

General Motor's conventional strategy of planned obsolescence ordained a strategic overhaul of the Camaro's appearance and chassis for the 1970 model year. The company's initial decision to go market with a simple exterior design surprised many executives within General Motors when the car became a big hit with buyers. This gave the engineers at Chevrolet time to refine the exterior without the criticism of a failed launch. They unleashed a surprise of their own by making considerable changes in the 1969 release, an uncommon move at the time, especially one year before a major redesign. The 1969 design became the most popular first-generation Camaro.

If Camaro was a home run in the first two years, the 1969 model was a walk-off grand slam. Most mechanical components were carried over from the previous years, while the exterior sheet metal was freshened up and reshaped with a sportier look. From nose to tail, the design looked more angled and aggressive. Inset headlights on the grille gave it a wedge-like shape. The sheet metal was formed to give the car a lower and wider appearance. This stance became known as "the hugger" model. The restyled dash and redesigned seats provided driver comfort at speed, but the biggest selling point was the staggering array of performance options. The five basic models supported 14 engine options.

This new look fit the racing image Chevrolet was carving out for its pony car. To avoid direct competition with other racing Chevrolets, Camaro targeted sports car racing. The Corvette was competing in the Le Mans series and the Chevelle had NASCAR tied up, so the Camaro was introduced into the SCCA Trans-Am racing series. Penske Racing's Mark Donohue won three races with the race-prepped version in 1967 before his

For the second time in three years, the Camaro SS model was selected as the pace car for the Indianapolis 500 race, an unprecedented but well-liked decision.

domination of the series in 1968, winning 10 races out of a 13-race season. Chevrolet knew that sales improved with each victory; it designed the 1969 Camaro to do even more damage in the Trans-Am series.

The 1969 Camaro backed up the Penske and Donohue 1968 championship by winning 8 of 12 races against a talent-filled field, including the Mustang team of Parnelli Jones and George Follmer. The public took notice of the Camaro's winning nature, which helped the 1969 model set production records that stood for a decade. On the dragstrip, Bill "Grumpy" Jenkins and Dick "Mr. Chevrolet" Harrell campaigned the Camaro SS from coast to coast with legendary success. The Camaro SS was chosen as the official pace car of the Indianapolis 500 for the second time, and pace car replicas were offered.

Although the Camaro was initially rushed to the showroom, these sporty coupes left a lasting legacy. Of the first-generation models, the final year is the automotive enthusiasts' favorite. Many experts consider the 1969 Camaro models the best of all time. Welburn surmised, "It didn't borrow from any other design and all these years later, it still looks fresh."

This book was written to help Camaro enthusiasts identify the high-performance SS Camaro models and the options available during the 1969 campaign. Understanding what parts were available, how they were numbered and identified, and which options were outfitted with those available parts is critical in appreciating this iconic machine.

The following chapters peel back the layers of the 1969 Camaro SS model, from the base SS 350 model to the legendary L89 special high-performance 396 Camaro SS, whose creation became the stuff of legend. Explaining the GM parts used, the documentation and codes on the cars, as well as what parts to look for, make this book a detailed look at the Camaro SS nameplate. The magic of the 1969 Camaro continues to breathe life into the latest iterations of the pony car, making it one of America's most beloved car styles.

ADVENT OF THE CAMARO SS

By the end of the 1960s, the Camaro concept cars of 1965 were just a dot in the Chevrolet designer's rearview mirror and the model was forging its own path through the world of auto styling. Unveiling a refined exterior for the new model year in 1969, Chevrolet left the horizontal panels of the roof and trunk lid virtually the same but added character lines on the body that gave the new model a streamlined look. Widening the fenders and quarter panels made the new Camaro appear lower and wider. Angular creases and modifications at the nose, fenders, and quarter panels along with molded creases from the rear of each wheel opening down the center of the body intensified the aggressive appearance.

HISTORY OF THE SUPER SPORT

General Motors' Super Sport, or SS, package made its first appearance for the 1961 Impala. The initial SS was a kit offered with any Impala, with a list price of $53.80. It included interior and exterior SS trim plus chassis reinforcements with an upgraded suspension of stronger springs and shocks. Power brakes were included along with narrow-band whitewall tires and spinner wheel covers. The interior was treated to a column-mounted 7,000-rpm tach and Corvette-style hand bar on the passenger-side dash. Only 453 of the 491,000 Impalas built in 1961 were ordered with the SS package.

Despite the lackluster sales of the package in Impala models, General Motors offered an SS package for the Chevy II in 1963 under RPO Z03, which fared better with 42,432 SS models of 372,626 units built. The package included special exterior emblems, an upgraded instrument package, wheel covers, side moldings, bucket seats, and a sporty floor shifter. This cost an additional $161.40,

The 1969 Camaro was the highest volume first-generation Camaro, selling 243,085 units in a long model run that extended from September 26, 1968, through the end of November 1969. Of those, 34,932 were SS models.

The 1968 two-segment taillight is on the right; the 1969 three-segment taillight is below. The addition of the three-segment taillight for the 1969 model year was a subtle change that added a depth to the look of the vehicle's rear by widening the car from behind.

(approximately $1,247.52 in 2015 U.S. currency).

Next was the Chevelle SS model, which became the turning point for the Super Sport legacy. The 1964 Chevelle SS is often considered GM's initial entry into the muscle car wars. The 1964–1965 Chevelles established the Super Sport as Chevrolet's signature performance option in the eyes of the public. The special Z16 Chevelle released in mid-1965 set the benchmark for high-performance upgrades with the big-block 396 engine upgrade. Only 201 Z16 Chevelles were built, yet these special high-performance editions set the stage for the SS396 models to become a series of their own in 1966 (with series style numbers 13817 and 13867).

The next milestone for the SS package came when Chevrolet unleashed the 1967 Camaro. Originally offered in Regular Production Option (RPO) codes that included a 350-ci V-8 engine option and the L35 and L78 396-ci big-block engine options, the 1967 Camaro SS captured the car-buying public's fancy. A convertible model was selected as the Indianapolis 500 pace car. The first year, the SS had non-functioning air inlets on the hood, as well as special striping and SS badging that enthusiasts had come to cherish. A total of 220,906 Camaros were produced in 1967 with 34,411 of those equipped with the SS package.

In 1968, the Camaro SS was earning legendary status, with many drag racers campaigning the big-block coupes in all regions of the country. No one considered them sleepers, and they did not disappoint in the pony car wars. Hood inserts designed to imitate velocity stacks were added to the SS models for 1968. Another major offering that year was an optional 350 hp 396-ci big-block. Several high-performance dealers, most notably Baldwin-Motion, Dana, and Yenko, began offering 427-ci big-block engines as a dealer-installed option. This set the stage for 1969, which became the most popular production year for the first-generation Camaro.

1969 CAMARO SS SPECS

Length	186.0 inches
Width	74.0 inches
Height	51.1 inches (coupe); 50.9 inches (convertible)
Wheelbase	108 inches
Curb Weight	3,145 pounds*
Front Track	59.6 inches
Rear Track	59.5 inches
Fuel Tank	18 gallons
Base Tires	F70 x 14 inches
Base Rims	14 x 7.00 (.40-inch offset)

* +/- 455, depending on engine and options.

The first-generation Camaro introduced the most recognizable emblems to enthusiasts. This "Camaro by Chevrolet" radiator grille header panel nameplate was a standard emblem on all 1969 models.

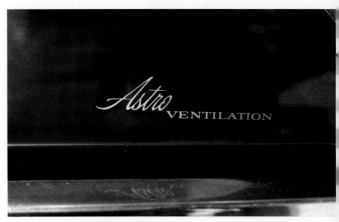

Wing windows were eliminated by virtue of the newly engineered Astro Ventilation airflow system.

1969 CAMARO BY THE NUMBERS

The following data was provided by General Motors Heritage Center.

Total Built	243,085
Coupes	225,512
6-Cylinder Coupes	34,541
V-8 Coupes	190,971
Convertibles	17,573
6-Cylinder Convertibles	1,707
V-8 Convertibles	15,866
SS Models	34,932
RS Models	37,773
Z/28 Models	20,302
Coupe Pace Cars	400 to 500*
Convertible Pace Cars	3,675
9560 COPO Models	69
9561 COPO Models	900 to 1,015**
9737 COPO Models	Unknown
9567 COPO Models	0

The 396 was a quick-revving and potent street engine with 325, 350, or 375 hp.

* Estimated based on Norwood production records.

** Estimated based on engine production totals for the year.

1969 Chevrolet Camaro SS
In Detail No. 4

MAJOR CHANGES IN 1969

In addition to the body lines, engineers made changes to the taillights by adding another segment making the unit a three-lens bezel. The nose grilles for all trim models got a more angular look with more openings. The faux louvers in the rear quarter panel (often called gills), added to the signature look. The interior received square gauges that complemented the lines of the car. Headrests became standard as part of ever-increasing federal safety regulations.

As in the two previous model years, the Camaro's F-Body chassis was uni-body construction from the firewall to the rear bumper. A steel-rail subframe was mounted to the front, which contained the engine and front suspension as well as mounts for the fenders, hood, and front support and bumper. The independent front suspension was composed of a double A-arm configuration; the rear suspension was a solid rear axle suspended by semi-elliptical leaf springs. Standard braking on a base model was supplied by four drum brakes.

The SS trim-level Camaros included Magic-Mirror lacquer paint, flush and dry rocker panels, curved side glass windows, dual-speed electric windshield wipers, built-in heater and defrost system, and carpeted floors. Every Camaro SS also included keyless locking of all doors, cushioned body mounting, an all-welded Fisher body, foot-operated parking brake, and an exhaust emissions control system. Standard Camaro emblems included "Camaro by Chevrolet" radiator grille,

header panel nameplate, and rear deck-lid; "Camaro" nameplates on doors, front fender nameplates, and the right-hand side of the instrument panel; bow-tie emblems on the rear panel and two-spoke plastic steering wheel with built-in horn tabs.

Other standard features included amber front side-marker lights with red rear side-marker lights, warning lights (for temperature, generator, oil pressure, and parking brake), driver-side outside rear-view mirror, seat belts for all passengers plus shoulder belts for the driver and front passenger. Vinyl headrests on the front seats became mandatory due to federal regulations. The new Astro Ventilation system eliminated the need for wing windows. Staggered rear shocks (one in front of the rear axle and one behind it) made a significant difference in handling by counteracting wheel hop under hard acceleration.

Typical model year production ran from August through July. The

Casting numbers were usually the first ones assigned by the chief engineer after pulling a block of numbers from Chevrolet's Central Office. Casting numbers earned their name because they were cast into parts at the foundry.

11

Advent of the Camaro SS
Chapter 1

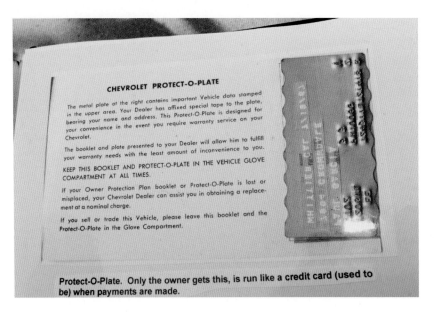

Protect-O-Plate. Only the owner gets this, is run like a credit card (used to be) when payments are made.

Vehicle identification and confirmation are determined with documents such as the Protect-O-Plate, broadcast sheets, VIN, and even the trim tag on the firewall. The more documentation you have, the clearer your understanding of how the vehicle left the assembly line.

1969 Camaro's popularity, combined with a manufacturing delay of the second-generation Camaro in 1970, led to an abnormally long production period extending into November 1969. A total of 243,085 Camaros were built during that extended production year. Chevrolet built 211,922 Camaros at the Norwood, Ohio, plant in 1969, with the additional 31,163 built in Van Nuys, California.

VEHICLE IDENTIFICATION

When it comes to understanding the 1969 Camaro SS, accurate vehicle identification is critical. Knowing the specifics of the car when it rolled off the assembly line helps in every aspect of the hobby, from restoration to customization. Supply and demand determines market values. Knowing exactly what you're looking at helps prevent a host of problems, such as being overcharged or being sold a fake.

Identification numbers on first-generation Camaros specify the equipment of a vehicle. General Motors didn't keep great records on every car and its options, but the Vehicle Identification Number (VIN), casting numbers, vehicle trim tag, and paperwork (window stickers, bill of sale, original invoice, broadcast sheets, etc.) can verify the details down to the original distributor model.

GM PART NUMBERING SYSTEM

A basic understanding of Chevrolet's part numbering system is critical when using the different codes and numbers to identify Camaro models and parts. During the 1960s, the Chevrolet Central Office in Warren, Michigan, controlled most administrative functions for marketing and sales. This included supplying seven-digit part numbers for all parts. This numbering system set aside blocks of numbers for future parts that the Engineering Group assigned to specific components or assemblies being designed.

The first entry in this block of numbers was usually the casting number (on the cylinder head or engine block). Next in the sequence was generally the machining number that was assigned to the component that required machining, such as a raw engine block. The next number represented the final assembly part number. The final set of sequential numbers represented each part that made up the completed assembly, including pistons, connecting rods, and crankshafts.

Casting numbers may have had alternative applications and been machined differently. An example is the popular "double hump" cylinder head on a 327-ci small-block 1968 Chevy. The number 3917291 was cast into the valve chest. This cylinder head was available with 1.94-inch intake valves (for the base 300-hp V-8 engine) or with larger 2.02-inch intake valves (for the optional 350-hp V-8 engine). The same casting number cylinder head was also manufactured with a hole for a temperature-sending unit when used on the 1968 Corvette models. Each of these raw castings was machined differently and therefore carried different GM part numbers.

Along with the GM casting numbers, date codes were cast into assemblies, which help with the identification process.

In addition to the part numbering system, the Central Office was also responsible for the RPO and COPO ordering systems.

VIN DECODING

The VIN is a 13-digit alpha-numeric code that gives general vehicle information. Each VIN is unique to its vehicle, just as fingerprints are to each person.

A federal law enacted in 1968 mandated that VIN plates be visible by law enforcement officials from outside the vehicle. The VIN plate for a 1969 Camaro was located on the top of the instrument panel, on the driver's side, and easily visible through the windshield.

An example of a 1969 Camaro VIN is 124379N605468. For Camaros, the first two digits in the VIN are always the same.

The first character indicates the GM manufacturer. In this case, it is a "1," which indicates Chevrolet Motor Division.

The second character signifies the model, a Camaro, which is represented by the number "2."

The third character signifies the engine type. A "3" designates a 6-cylinder engine and a "4" indicates that an 8-cylinder engine was installed. Unfortunately, General Motors did not use coding to indicate the specific engine, only the type of engine.

The fourth and fifth characters are used to designate the body style. Only two body styles were available for the Camaro: coupé or convertible. The number "37" in the fourth and fifth places in the VIN denotes a two-door hardtop coupe and a "67" is used for the two-door convertible coupe.

The sixth character defines the model year. The last digit in the year is used; therefore a 1969 Camaro always has a number "9" in this spot.

The character in the seventh position of the VIN identifies the assembly plant. Camaros were only built in two plants in

By 1969, federal regulations required a vehicle's VIN to be visible from outside the car. In most vehicles, including the 1969 Camaro, the VIN is visible through the driver's side of the windshield. The VIN provides general vehicle information and no two are the same.

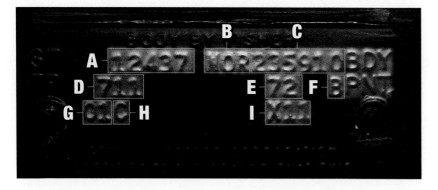

The trim tags were similar between the Norwood and Los Angeles (Van Nuys) assembly plants. The vehicle's body number was unique to each car and controlled by Chevrolet's Central Office. Norwood trim tags included the famous X-codes. These were added mid-year (during the second week of December) as an aid for the assembly workers. This code identified body trim and paint changes for the various Camaro models.

1969. The letter "N" is for Camaros built in Norwood, Ohio, and the letter "L" (Los Angeles) is for vehicles assembled in Van Nuys, California.

The final six digits in the VIN represent the specific unit number of the vehicle. This is a sequential number starting with 500001 at each plant for 1969. The next car assembled was given the next number in sequence making each VIN unique. Although two cars can have the same sequence number (one from Norwood and the other from Van Nuys), no two cars can have the same exact VIN.

TRIM PLATES

The VIN can provide a lot of general information about a vehicle, but trim plates also can offer detailed information about the scheduled original build of the car. Many vehicle specific details such as interior and exterior color, style, and trim are contained on this data plate.

Although the plant attempted to keep every detail correct, there were numerous instances where a specific paint code was listed on the trim plate, but the vehicle was not finished with that paint code.

Mistakes on the assembly line, customer requests, and product shortages on the line gave way to discrepancies in the trim plate and the actual finished vehicle. Despite these fairly common mistakes, the trim plate is recognized as one of the best sources of information for a specific vehicle in lieu of the actual broadcast sheet. It is often referred to as "the build sheet."

The 1969 Camaro trim plate is a small aluminum tag riveted to the engine firewall, on the driver's side above the master brake cylinder. The trim tag had different styles through the years, so it is important to understand what model and year is being decoded.

"Body by Fisher" heads had the 1969 trim tag as an embossed title. This establishes the Fisher body assembly plant as responsible for the information on the trim tag.

Directly below that is the style and body line, which contains the body style code and the assembly plant code. The next line indicates the interior trim and exterior paint codes.

The third and final embossed line contains the body build date code and other body-related option codes, including the famous Norwood assembly plant's X-codes for Camaros.

THE FIVE CAMARO MODELS OF 1969

Part of the appeal of the 1969 Camaro was the single-year styling and the fact that a customer could choose so many options among the five basic models. Chevrolet offered 13 engine options

The V-8 engine for the base model Camaro SS was an L48 350-ci small-block Chevy rated at 300 hp.

alone, not counting the L72 big-block powerplants destined for the secretive COPO models. There was something for everyone, from the budget-friendly base models in either the sport coupe or convertible to the performance-minded Z/28 package or Super Sport models. This book focuses on the SS cars fitted with base 350- and 396-ci engines.

The base V-8 engine at the beginning of the model run was the 327-ci LF7. This was replaced by the 307-ci L14 in January 1969. The 350-ci LM1 with a 4-barrel carburetor was the optional base V-8 engine early in the production run. Like the base V-8 engine, the LM1 was also replaced in January 1969 by the L65 350-ci V-8.

The Saginaw M15 3-speed manual transmission was the base transmission for the non–high-performance V-8 engines. For the LM1 engine, the heavy-duty Muncie 3-speed was required if another transmission was not ordered. The 2-speed Powerglide and the more popular TH350 were optional automatic transmissions for the base model V-8 platforms.

Every 1969 Camaro was equipped with bucket seats, rear bumper guards, and an 11/16-inch front sway bar for the small-block. Disc brakes and a 4-speed manual transmission were available on any 1969 Camaro as an option.

Convertible models were equipped with a folding convertible top, and a power-operated convertible top

was optional. Unlike sport coupes, the convertible models didn't have color-coordinated roof rails, shoulder belt clips, coat hooks, plastic seat belt anchor covers, or a dome light. Due to the folding top, the shoulder belt molding was in the rear, courtesy lights were under the instrument panel, and the windshield pillars received bright moldings with bright windshield header and convertible top latches.

The convertible's sun visors were narrower and radio speakers were installed in the front kick panels. The rear inside body panels had built-in armrests and ashtrays.

The 1969 Camaro convertible models are distinctly different than the sport coupes. There was no dome light, sun visors were narrowed, radio speakers were mounted in the front kick panels, and many other changes were made. This particular convertible has the Rally Sport option that features hidden headlights, striping package, and upgraded wheels, bucket seats, and carpeting.

CONVERTIBLE VIBRATION DAMPENER PART NUMBERS

Location	GM Part Number
Front Driver's Side	3950101
Front Passenger's Side	3950102
Rear Driver's Side	3950109
Rear Passenger's Side	3950110

Vibration dampeners were installed on all four corners of the convertible Camaro to help eliminate body oscillation caused by chassis flex at speed. Mounted vertically on each side of the trunk, these dampeners resembled cocktail shakers.

The convertible body styles were equipped with E78 x 14–inch tires and a strengthening floor brace.

Convertible Camaros inherited a flexible body due to the lack of a roof and supporting structure. Engineers added reinforcement around the rockers and floor area, which helped reduce some of the body flex. Despite the added reinforcement, an inherent oscillating vibration manifested in the chassis at speed. To lessen the vibration and smooth out ride quality, GM engineers added vibration dampeners at all four corners of the chassis. These vibration dampeners were installed on all first-generation convertible Camaros.

Commonly referred to as "cocktail shakers," due to their appearance and function, the dampeners consisted of a weighted mass suspended on a spring inside a large can filled with a viscous fluid. Each dampener weighed about 25 pounds. Designed to absorb the energy caused by the body's oscillations, the dampeners were tuned to the resonant frequency at which the vibrations existed.

RALLY SPORT PACKAGE

The Rally Sport (RS) appearance package could be added to any Camaro model, including the 6-cylinder base model. Not considered a performance package, the RS RPO (Z22) included the exterior style trim group Z21 RPO features along with several unique trim features for which the RS package had become famous in the first two model years. Adding the RS features to any model effectively bumped the original body style to

the next level. Because nothing in the VIN or trim tag specifically identifies a vehicle as an RS model, the package features have been added to standard models over the years to pass off as original RS models.

The Z21 trim package included the bright moldings for the wheelwell openings and drip rail (on the coupe) rear fender louvers, fender pinstriping, and black body sill. The featured trim items exclusive to the RS package were the signature RS grille with concealed headlights, backup lights located below the rear bumper, special taillights, and headlight washers. Emblems identifying the car as an RS were attached to the grille, fender, fuel cap, and tail panel. RS horn buttons were also included on certain steering wheels.

The retractable headlamp doors of the 1969 package were restyled to include "peek-a-boo" slots. These slots allowed light to shine through the door ensuring that the driver had visibility at night if the door failed to retract. For the first and only time, the 1969 Camaro RS package included headlight washers. They were offered as a stand-alone option on non-RS Camaros, but very few were sold. A total of 37,773 Rally Sport packages (Z22) were produced.

The first-generation Camaros are known for some of the most recognizable emblems in automotive history. The 1969 Camaro was the first, and only, first-generation Camaro to wear the Rally Sport nameplate. This was mounted on both front fenders behind the wheelwell openings.

The SS and SS/RS models were instantly identified by the black grille and black tail panel. Other models sported a silver grille and body-colored tail panel.

CHAPTER 2

CAMARO SS AND SPECIAL EDITION CARS

First-generation Camaros have achieved special interest status with most car enthusiasts and collectors. This is especially true of the 1969 Camaro due to the sporty exterior design change that made the 1969 model year easily recognizable. Even the most basic 1969 Camaro is worth much more today than when it drove off the showroom floor new. Although 1969 Camaros in general garner attention, collectors and enthusiasts cherish the SS and special models for their rarity and place in history. These cars command attention and premium prices on the collector car market.

In addition to the special, rare, optioned Camaros, the Indianapolis 500 Pace Car editions are high on any collector's list. The 1969 model year also saw the birth of a high-performance Camaro with a factory-installed aftermarket engine, purpose-built for racing, through the little-known COPO program. Only 69 of these ZL1 aluminum-engine COPO Camaros were built, which made this model legendary as soon as the first batch left the assembly plant. The COPO Camaros are not covered in depth in this book, but they warrant mention by virtue of the fact that they were built on the SS platform.

The Z11 Indy Pace Car Edition convertible was designed to grab and hold your attention. It was a festival car that served many roles during the Indy 500, including carrying qualifying drivers during the Indy parade. The cars were Dover White RS/SS convertibles with Hugger Orange Z28-style stripes with an orange hound's-tooth cloth seat interior. (Photo Courtesy Classic Industries)

The 1969 Camaro SS models had larger, more powerful engines with heavy-duty suspensions to match.

CAMARO SUPER SPORT

Super Sport, also known as "the one with the name like the hiss of a snake," was the signature performance package of Chevrolet, especially in the 1960s. When it came to the Camaro, Chevrolet added the performance option but did not call it the Super Sport; it was simply SS. More than just trim, the first-generation Camaro SS models had larger, more powerful engines with suspensions that were beefed up to match that power. The engine options for SS models included the small-block 350-ci L48 rated at 300 hp up to the

Z27 CAMARO SS PRODUCTION

Engine Type	Vehicles Manufactured
L65 250 hp 350 ci	26,898
L48 300 hp 350 ci	22,339
L35 325 hp 396 ci	6,752
L34 350 hp 396 ci	2,018
L78 375 hp 396 ci	4,889
L89 375 hp 396 ci	311

five big-block 396-ci engines. The 396 big-blocks included a 350-hp L34, 325-hp L33, 295-hp L48, 375-hp L78, and L78 with aluminum heads that held the L89 designation.

The base engine in the SS package was the L48 350-ci small-block, which was automatically deleted when a big-block 396-ci engine was selected. Dual exhaust, a performance clutch, and the Muncie M21 transmission with a 12-bolt rear axle housing completed the powertrain combination. The upgraded suspension comprised heavy-duty springs, front power disc brakes, special ball joints, performance front springs and shocks, and upgraded F70 x 14–inch raised white-letter tires. A heavy-duty radiator was required with the performance engines along with a high-torque starter, special hood with hood insulation, and engine mounts for the larger block.

The distinctive badges and stripes, along with the iconic black tail panel, made the SS models easily identifiable. In addition to the black tail panel, SS models received a black grille instead of the standard silver grille as on other models. Available in the sport coupe and convertible body styles, performance-minded hot rodders favored SS models because of the obvious power upgrades.

In 1969, the Camaro was selected as the Indianapolis 500 pace car for the second time; the 1967 Camaro had been selected previously.

Sales of the 1969 Camaro were robust, due in part to the long production year. Some 1969 Camaros were sold in 1970 as 1970 models. This caused a problem when the second-generation Camaros hit the market, so these were designated 1970½ Camaros.

General Motors used a couple of 1969 model Camaros in some early advertisements for the 1970 models, leading to more confusion and accusations of using "left over" Camaros as new cars. Even with the confusion, the basic five models of the 1969 Camaro sold more than the other first-generation models.

INDIANAPOLIS 500 PACE CAR AND PACE CAR REPLICA

Starting with the first race in 1911, a pace car has been used during the Indianapolis 500. Known as "The Greatest Spectacle in Racing," the Indy 500 had truly become the most popular auto race in America by 1969. Every aspect of the event was covered by the press and consumed by the fans, usually on tape delay broadcast on ABC or on live radio broadcast with legendary announcer Sid Collins. Steeped in tradition, the festival surrounding the event highlighted the latest innovations in racing and the automotive industry, which made the selection of the official pace car an important event. Indianapolis officials attempted to vary the selection of the pace car across the various auto manufacturers, with an emphasis on performance vehicles. This method was used for pace car selection until 2002 when Chevrolet became the exclusive auto manufacturer to provide the pace car and support vehicles for the event.

In 1969, for the second time in three years, a Camaro was selected as the

1969 Chevrolet Camaro SS
In Detail No. 4

official pace car of the race. The 1967 Camaro was celebrated for the style and innovations in a newly released vehicle. In 1969, the Camaro was chosen again due to its performance. Car manufacturers fought hard for the privilege to be selected, and no car in the post-war era (1945–1978) had been selected twice for the honor, not even the Corvette.

Indianapolis Motor Speedway president Tony Hulman, along with Pete Estes, then president of the Chevrolet division of General Motors, announced the 1969 pace car choice to an eager public. Estes went on to become president of General Motors four years later. The January announcement included a general description of the car: a white exterior with orange stripes on the Camaro RS/SS, with an orange interior and ducted hood.

For their part, Chevrolet agreed to provide 130 pace car replicas in addition to the two official pace cars and one replica pace car for the race winner. These 130 cars were part of the support fleet for the event, which also included 16 Impala station wagons, 18 Chevrolet pickups, two Suburban trucks, and one van. The Indy committee received 43 of these Camaros as festival cars for the festival queens and other dignitaries to be driven around the track in during the event. All received a special gold festival decal on the side.

Another 75 replicas were assigned to the VIP/press fleet. Five of the replicas were assigned to USAC, the sanctioning body for the race, and an additional seven replicas were given to Indianapolis

Motor Speedway for official speedway use. In comparison, only 81 Camaro pace cars were built as support and courtesy cars in 1967.

THE OFFICIAL PACE CARS

Only two 1969 Indianapolis 500 pace cars were specially built. They started as typical SS Camaro convertible body style with the N40 power steering package with quick-ratio steering, the N34 sport-styled steering wheel with wood-grain plastic trim, and the D55 center console with U17 special instrumentation package and AM radio. These were shipped directly from the Norwood assembly plant to the GM Tech Center in Warren, Michigan, where Chevrolet's Engineering Division and the Experimental Department prepared them for the race.

These cars were designed specifically for pacing duties with a high-performance drivetrain that was stacked with the 396-ci, 375-hp L89 engine. For absolute dependability, the team removed the L89 aluminum cylinder heads, and replaced them with the L78 cast-iron high-performance heads. The engines were completely disassembled, blueprinted, inspected, Magnafluxed, and dye penetrant–inspected before being reassembled. Chevrolet took great care to ensure that the drivetrain could withstand the rigors of the safety car job.

Not leaving anything to chance, the engineers selected the heavy-duty Turbo-Hydramatic 400 transmission (M40), which received the same disassembly, inspection, and blueprinting

OPPOSITE:
The Z11 Indy Pace Car Edition convertible is a great piece of Camaro and Indianapolis 500 history. Returning as the pace car in 1969 after holding pace car honors in 1967, the Camaro SS featured the white with Hugger Orange stripes. It is one of the most popular Indy pace cars of all time.

as the engine. The final touch was the addition of a special high-performance six-bolt torque converter used on the 427-ci COPO Camaros. These pace cars received the heavy-duty rear end with 3.31 gears and the F41 suspension components including special front and rear springs and matching shock absorbers. The rear-end gears were shotpeened for strength, Magnafluxed and inspected for stressors or flaws, and heat treated. The heavy-duty driveshaft was dynamically balanced to ensure smooth operation at pacing speeds. Driveline failure was not an option and Chevrolet engineers made sure their cars were not going to flop on the biggest stage in auto racing.

The engineering team beefed up the electrical system by adding a heavy-duty battery (T60), heavy-duty alternator (K85), temperature-controlled fan clutch, and heavy-duty radiator (V01) to this special use vehicle. The front drive belts were "pre-stretched" to make sure that they didn't stretch and fly off the pulleys at 130 mph, the expected speed of the pace car. Hoses were attached with "aircraft-style" ratcheting-type hose clamps that self-locked for that extra measure of security.

Front JL8 disc brakes were also added at the tech center. Rear JL8 axles were installed and the rear disc brakes were used. The stock 14-inch wheels were removed and replaced with the larger-diameter 15-inch Rally wheels. One car was fitted with special Goodyear tires and the other received Firestone tires, which gave both manufacturers equal representation during the event.

Modifications made specifically for pace car duties included passenger grab handles above the rear-seat armrests and flag-pole mounting brackets on the rear bumper to hold the yellow warning flags. Mounting the flag-pole brackets required 1968 exhaust tips instead of 1969 exhaust tips. A two-way radio was installed for communication between the occupants of the pace car and the control tower. Fasteners to hold the convertible top in place were added along with hood pins to lock the hood in place.

Former 1960 Indy 500 winner and Chevrolet dealer Jim Rathmann was chosen to drive the pace car with starter Tony Hulman and astronaut Pete Conrad as passengers. Pace car number 1 was used to start the race and pace car number 2 was used to restart the race after a yellow-flag stoppage.

Eventually, both cars were acquired by private parties and are in private collections today. As of this writing, Vernon Smith of Newfoundland owns pace car number 1 and Wade Ogle of California owns pace car number 2.

RACE WINNER REPLICA

By tradition, the race winner is presented with a replica of the pace car. It was good marketing strategy to have an Indianapolis 500 winner driving in a particular model car. Chevrolet wanted its latest popular nameplate in the hands of the race winner. The first time a Camaro was awarded the pace car honors in 1967, race winner A. J. Foyt turned down the pace car replica citing the absence of air

Door decals were shipped in the trunk of the replicas, allowing the new owners the option of installing the decals or not.

Restored 1969 Camaro pace cars are very collectable and can be seen at larger car shows. This one was professionally restored by Quality Muscle Car Restorations, in Scottsdale, Arizona.

conditioning and a power top. Chevrolet decided to produce another car for Foyt through a run of special Canadian-built cars.

Unwilling to suffer the same embarrassing rejection, Chevrolet assembled the winner's pace car replica with a show car finish, air conditioning, and a power top. Mario Andretti won the race, and the car, which he gave to his brother Aldo. The location of this car is unknown, but rumors persist that the car was sold and shipped to New Zealand.

FESTIVAL CARS

The 43 designated festival cars and courtesy cars for the Speedway and invited celebrities were equipped with 350-ci V-8 engines and automatic transmissions. Many of these were used for events that required a festival queen or other dignitary sitting on the rear deck waving to the spectators. Deciding to

use automatic transmissions in these vehicles prevented the accidental ejection of a dignitary or festival queen if an inexperienced driver popped the clutch and launched the car. Festival car number 34 (VIN 9N609349) was part of the gifts awarded to Janet Lee Faires Kendall for fulfilling her duties as queen of the festival.

The other 116 cars that were provided as official speedway and USAC cars, were configured in different powertrain arrangements with most having either the 396-ci big-block engines with 4-speed manual transmission or 350-ci engines with automatic transmissions.

Z11 PACE CAR REPLICAS

Designed to be visible at a busy racetrack, the pace car paint scheme used many existing Camaro options. The new Hugger Orange paint was used in hood and decklid stripes to contrast with the

Modifications specifically for the pace car included passenger hand holds, front and rear.

This Camaro 396 SS/RS in Hugger Orange carries the Rally wheels with original Goodyear Polyglas tires. In 1969, Chevy produced 34,932 SS Camaros, and 15,573 convertibles rolled off the assembly line.

A perfectly restored 350SS pace car engine complete with proper smog control items.

Arctic White exterior paint. The SS stripes were dropped in favor of the Z/28 hood and decklid stripes. The pace cars and the replicas were the only non-Z/28 models to receive the rally stripes. In addition to dropping the SS stripes, the black tail pan indicating a big-block engine was also omitted, along with the blacked-out rocker panels, which were white on the replicas. Chevrolet planned to use the Indianapolis 500 exposure to sell the replicas and announce a special model.

In a confidential GM product bulletin dated February 4, 1969, the new Z11 RPO code vehicle was introduced, being "comprised of a Camaro SS/Rally Sport (Camaro SS RPO Z27 with Rally Sport equipment RPO Z22)." The bulletin also identified some "exceptions" to be adhered to under the limited run:

- Hugger Orange hood and decklid paint stripes, same as RPO Z28
- White body sill instead of black
- White rear panel instead of black, as specified with 396 V-8 engine options
- Removal of sport striping (reference RPO D90)
- Addition of Hugger Orange fender striping (reference RPO D96, part of RPO Z22)
- Exterior body color, Dover White, Code 911

This 350 SS Camaro Convertible was bumped up the hierarchy with the addition of the RS option, making it a very desirable 350 Camaro SS/RS.

The RS appearance package included hidden headlights with badging and exterior bright trim.

The RS package was available on any Camaro model, but was spectacular when added to the SS Camaro.

One of the most signature changes in 1969 was the RS revised backup lights under the rear bumper.

The bulletin went on to detail the custom interior as RPO Z87 with the exception that Orange hound's-tooth cloth trim, code 720, would be used. An air-induction hood (RPO ZL2) and Rally wheel, hubcap, and trim ring (RPO ZJ7) were also specified in the construction.

General Motors identified additional mandatory options in the replica cars to make them identical to the actual pace cars. These options included:

- M40 Turbo-Hydramatic
- G80 Posi-Traction rear axle
- N40 Power steering
- C06 Power convertible top
- D55 Console
- U17 Special instrumentation
- U63 AM Radio
- D80 Air spoiler, front and rear
- N34 Sport styled steering wheel
- YA1 Custom deluxe seat and front shoulder belts (A39 and A85)
- A01 Soft-Ray tinted glass

Chevrolet offered pace car replicas with the intent of producing one for each Chevrolet dealership amounting to 6,400 across the United States. In the end, only 3,675 replicas were produced, including the Camaros that saw action as courtesy and festival cars at the Indianapolis 500. Despite the mandatory options spelled out in the product bulletin, the Z11 pace car replicas were all RS/SS convertibles with a base drivetrain consisting of the SS350 with a 3-speed manual transmission. Engine upgrade options and transmission options were available, but the 396-ci engine with 4-speed transmission was the most popular.

Unfortunately, records are not available of the exact configurations of each Z11 manufactured. The door decals were included from the factory and shipped in the trunk. Some dealers installed the decals, but most door decals were installed, based on owner choice.

Z10 PACE CAR

A limited number of RS/SS pace car coupes were made and sold in the Southwest with no explanation for the limited availability. At first, experts thought these were custom made by fans liking the pace car look but in a coupe. As time went by and more showed up, enthusiasts discovered these were factory-made cars. The Z10 replicas were duplicates of the original pace cars, right down to the paint scheme, except in coupe versions.

As with many special versions during this timeframe, poor records and incomplete data from the manufacturer have left the automotive community without solid evidence of the production numbers for the Z10. Production estimates from experts place the number of Z10 actually manufactured around 400. In all these years, not one document has been uncovered explaining why these units were produced. Like the Z11 replicas, the Z10 coupes (including the 396-ci cars) were Dover White with white rocker panels and tail panels. All Z10s came with RPO D80 front and rear spoilers, rally wheels, and the specially ducted hood (RPO ZL2). According to the Camaro Research Group, experts in first-generation Camaros,

High-performance dealerships, including Nickey's Chevrolet in Chicago, were known for performing upgrades on stock Camaros with performance parts approved and sold by Chevrolet. Many of these dealerships worked with successful drag racer/builders such as Dick Harrell to further tune these performance Camaros.

there is no evidence that any Z10 coupes were manufactured with the orange hound's-tooth interior as with the Z11 pace car replicas. Only five interiors were installed in Z10 coupes: the standard ivory, black standard, black deluxe, black hound's-tooth, and ivory hound's-tooth.

The L48 350-ci 295-hp base SS engine is found in most known Z10s. The optional L35 396-ci 325-hp has been found in a few existing Z10s, and a few L78 396-ci 375-hp engines have also been documented. A 3-speed manual transmission was the standard base for the Z10 coupe with optional automatic and 4-speed transmissions available. As with other RS/SS cars, air conditioning was an option fitted to most Z10s that left the factory. They did not come with door decals; they were not installed at the

dealers. Although they are considered a coupe version of the pace car replicas, they are not hardtop versions of the Z11 pace car replicas. They are very rare.

DEALER-MODIFIED CAMARO SS MODELS

A handful of Chevrolet dealers modified Camaro SS models for more performance. These dealers worked with Chevrolet's performance division, purchasing more powerful engines from the factory, and transplanting these big-blocks into the Camaro's lightweight chassis for amazing street/strip performance. By 1969, these high-performance dealers found a "back door" enabling them to order special engine combinations normally reserved for fleet vehicles such as ambulances.

Classic Industries' car collection includes a very rare 1969 Dick Harrell–built L72 Camaro. It is one of ten that Harrell built in 1969.

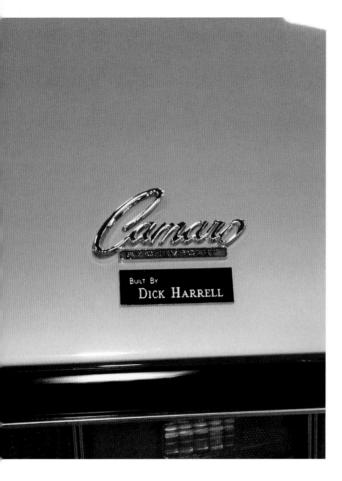

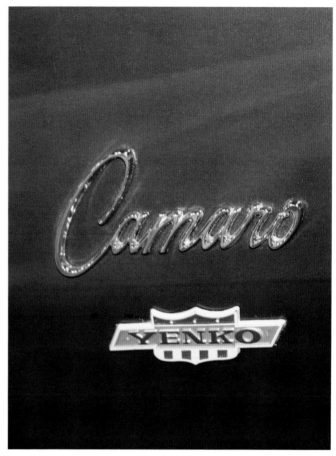

The Central Office Production Order (COPO) process became the revolutionary method for ordering cars never intended for production. First used by dealer Fred Gibb in Illinois, the COPO process was perfected by Don Yenko of Yenko Chevrolet in Pennsylvania. Yenko worked with Chevrolet performance to have modifications performed at the factory to reduce amount of labor required by the dealer for modification. Because the cars were made at the factory, they qualified for factory racing series, and dominated at the tracks.

In addition to Gibb and Yenko, several other dealerships performed these modifications and sold COPO models for Camaro enthusiasts who wanted to race. Of those, the most notable were Baldwin-Motion Chevrolet in Baldwin, New York; Berger Chevrolet in Grand Rapids, Michigan; Dana Chevrolet in South Gate, California; Nickey Chevrolet in Chicago, Illinois; and Scuncio Chevrolet in Greenville, Rhode Island. These dealerships typically added performance items such as headers and appearance packages resulting in turnkey race-prepped cars for the public.

These high-performance Camaros often gave little indication of their performance under the hood. A simple emblem attached to the hood, grille, or trunk was the only clue given to the competition.

The legendary ZL1 all-aluminum 427-ci big-block, rated at 425 hp, and the Yenko L72 iron-block 427 big-blocks are considered the quickest and most valuable Camaro engines ever built. Only 69 ZL1s were manufactured in 1969. The Yenko and Harrell versions were only slightly more plentiful.

Chevrolet had a variety of engine options available in the early 1960s for muscle car and potential Camaro customers. By the time the 1969 Camaro was released, Chevrolet produced a mind-blowing 14 engine options in the line. Everything from the economical 230-ci inline 6-cylinder that produced a modest 140 hp to the 427-ci ZL1 V-8 pushing 430 hp, making the COPO Camaro one of the quickest cars of the decade.

The differences between the engines were as unique as the trim levels.

There were three major categories: two 6-cylinder engines, six small-block V-8 engines, and six big-block V-8s. The SS models were available with one of five engines; an L48 350-ci 295-hp small-block; or one of four big-block engines: L35 396-ci 325-hp, L34 396-ci 350-hp, L78 396-ci 375-hp, or L89 396-ci 375-hp.

All Chevrolet engines have several codes cast or stamped into the block for identification. The casting is done during the foundry process. Other markings, such as the engine ID code, are stamped into the block on a pad specially made for that purpose. V-8 engines are stamped on the pad just forward of the passenger-side cylinder head. Casting numbers are near the bellhousing flange on the V-8 blocks. These codes accurately identify engines and their components.

SMALL-BLOCK ENGINES

General Motors' 1960s small-block engines are the stuff of legends. Inexpensive and cheap to maintain, these small-blocks were used in virtually every Chevrolet mid-size and full-size car and truck model. Most appropriately, Ed Cole, the man credited with developing the small-block Chevy engine, was also involved with the COPO Camaro program. As the President of GM's

ROCHESTER CARBURETOR ID NUMBER

Shown here is the breakdown.

First three digits	702 = 1960s
Fourth digit	9 = 1969
Fifth digit	0 = Monojet
	1 = Two-jets
	2 = Quadrajet
	3 = Monojet
	4 = Two-jets
	5 = Quadrajet
	6 = Varijet
Sixth digit	1 = Chevrolet
Seventh digit	Even number = Auto transmission
	Odd number = Manual transmission

Dick Harrell was instrumental in bringing the ZL1 into being, but when it came time to build his own branded SS Camaro, he settled on the 427-spec iron block for reliability.

car and truck group, Cole controlled which dealers were invited into the high-performance program. The first generation of small-block Chevy engines solidified Cole's career by becoming the most popular engine in Chevrolet's history. This popularity extended into 1969 when the Camaro was offered in six variants of the small-block engine in both high- and low-output versions. Only one small-block Chevy engine was available in the SS model.

Chevrolet small- and big-block engines have casting numbers in the rear of the block where the transmission mounts, at the very top of the block, facing up. Engine block casting numbers give a clue to the vehicle's history. Different casting numbers were produced throughout the manufacturing season.

Similarities and Differences

Except for the Z28 302-ci engine, all small-block Camaro engines used the same alternator. Vehicles without air conditioning were equipped with a 37-amp base unit (PN 1100834) and those with air conditioning used the 61-amp (PN 1100843). All small-blocks used a standard Delco-Remy voltage regulator (PN 6272157).

The camshaft used in all small-blocks, except the Z28 302-ci high-performance engine, carried, casting number 3896930 (PN 3896929). This hydraulic lifter camshaft had a lift of .390/.410 (intake/exhaust) and duration of 310/320 (intake/exhaust). The Z28 engine was fitted with a solid lifter camshaft, casting number 3849347 (PN 3849346) with a lift of .485/.485 (intake/exhaust) and duration of 346/346 (intake/exhaust).

All small-block engines installed in the 1969 Camaro had the same firing order, 1-8-4-3-6-5-7-2, which was standard for all first-generation small-block Chevy engines.

SMALL-BLOCK: BLOCK AND CYLINDER HEAD CASTING NUMBERS

Small-Block Engine	Block Casting Number	Cylinder Head Casting Number
Z28 302 ci/290 hp	3932386 (four-bolt)	3927186
	3956618 (four-bolt)	3947041
	3970010 (four-bolt)	3947041
L65 350 ci/250 hp	3956618 (two-bolt)	3932441
LM1 350 ci/255 hp	3956618 (two-bolt)	3932441
L48 350 ci/295 hp (SS Engine Option)	3932386 (four-bolt)	3947041
	3956618 (four-bolt)	3927186
	3970010 (four-bolt)	3947041

CHEVY 350-CI SMALL-BLOCK SS ENGINE OPTIONS

The 350-ci small-block was introduced in the 1967 Camaro, which forever tied the two together as a staple for a couple of decades. The L48 350 small-block Chevy is the original performance 350. Originally offered in the 1967 Super Sport Camaro, the L48 thrived until 1980 when it was discontinued in the Corvette C3 series.

The L48 engine package was also used in the Nova line through 1979 with a few changes over the years. In 1969, however, the L48 engine was used in practically every mid-size and many full-size Chevrolet models. The power output was a respectable 300 hp with 380 ft-lbs of torque and a compression ratio of 10.25:1.

L48 350-CI 295-HP

The L48 engine used the same 4-barrel carburetors (Rochester 4-barrel), cast-iron intake manifold (PN 3927184) and transmission as the LM1 engine

The first-generation small-block Chevy 350 is one of the most popular small-block engines of all time and is credited as one of the top engine designs ever.

The L48 350-ci small-block sold 22,339 copies in 1969, which represented just under 10 percent of the Camaros equipped with the engine for the model year.

option. The difference between the two engines was in the cylinder head. The L48 heads had a significantly smaller, 63-cc, combustion chamber compared to the LM1's 76-cc chamber. This gave the L48 a higher compression ratio of 10.25:1 and a major increase in power.

The engine internals were the same for both the L48 and LM1, but the distributors were different due to higher compression and distributor calibration. A larger 2.25-inch exhaust system was used, which differed from other 350-ci engines using a 2-inch-diameter exhaust. The L48 represented 9 percent of the total Camaros sold in 1969 with 22,339 making their way into the public's hands.

Small-block improvements in the 350-ci engine included a larger main journal (2.45-inch) with improved webbing in the block and main bearing saddles for improved strength. Both two- and four-bolt main bearing engine blocks were used during the 1969 model year. The main caps were made of gray iron with a few instances of nodular iron caps in high-horsepower engines. Nodular iron caps have the letter "N" cast into the cap. Cylinder heads made before the 1969 model year were not drilled and tapped for accessory mounting bolts.

The connecting rods used in all 350-ci engines were 5.7-inch center-to-center (PN 3916396), forged-steel construction with 3/8-inch rod bolts, and pressed-pin

piston design. Like other small-blocks, the 350-ci blocks used a 1-5/8-inch-diameter freeze plug set (PN 3826504). The rear cam plug on all 1969 small-blocks was the same (PN 10241154), with cup plugs (PN 14091563) for the lifter galleries. Cam bearings for the first-generation 350-ci engines were the same; the first bearing (PN 474005), the second and fifth bearings (PN 474006), and the third and fourth (PN 474007) bearings fit into their respective positions based on size.

BIG-BLOCK ENGINES

The 1969 model year marked the last production year for the 396-ci Mark IV big-block. Second-generation production Camaros with "396SS" badges were sold in the following years but carried 402-ci engines. All four of the true 396-ci engines offered in 1969 shared the 4.094-inch bore and 3.76-inch stroke but with different horsepower configurations.

The 396-inch engine was originally designed and introduced in the 1965 Corvette C2 as the L78 engine option. Added quickly as an experimental Z16 package on the 1965 Chevelle chassis, the mechanical solid lifter version could spin into the high-6,000 range. Rated at 425 hp in the Corvette, this became the staple muscle car engine for General Motors for the rest of the decade.

The 427-ci big-block was the king of engines for the 1969 Camaro. They instantly became high-performance models handled by special dealerships that dealt in performance. This is an L89 COPO 427.

Known for their rugged design with sturdy main bearing caps and a forged-steel crankshaft in high-performance models, these big-blocks are considered by many to be the most reliable large-displacement V-8 engines of all time. These big-blocks are generally divided into two categories: low-performance big-blocks (L-35 and L-34) and high-performance big-blocks (L78, L89, and L72). The ZL1 big-block is in a league of its own.

Three big-block casting numbers were used in 1969. The 3935440 casting number blocks were excess blocks from 1968 that were used in the beginning of the 1969 model year. Casting number 3955272 blocks were the primary 396-ci big-block used in Camaros that year. At the end of the production run, casting number 3969854 was used. This casting signified the beginning of the 402-ci big-blocks (essentially a 396-ci overbored 0.030-inch). This was common in 1970 models.

The performance 396-ci engines were drilled and tapped for four-bolt main bearing caps. The L35 and L34 received two-bolt main bearing caps. All 396-ci and 427-ci big-block engines received chrome valvecovers with oil drippers on the inside to help lubricate the rocker arms. The 1969 big-block engines also received a newly designed water pump, spaced farther away from the timing cover than in the previous year. Two casting numbers identified the new water pumps, 3969811 and 3931065, without regard to engine RPO.

All 1969 big-block Camaros were equipped with the Air Injection Reactor (AIR) pollution control system. The AIR system consisted of an air pump (casting number 7801149), located on the passenger's side of the engine, the same as on small-block models. Two smog tube assemblies were available, one for each cylinder head bank, and a diverter valve (PN 7029297). The solid lifter big-block engines were fitted with a deep-groove pulley on the air pump (PN 3932458) and the low-performance big-block engines received a shallow groove pulley (PN 3927116). The big-block AIR pump mounting bracket carries PN 3940945.

All big-block electrical systems used the standard GM voltage regulator (PN 6272159) with different amperage charging systems. The same exhaust manifolds were used for all big-block engines with PN 3909879 on the driver's side and PN 3916178 on the driver's side. A Delco-Remy starter (PN 1108418) was used on all big-block Camaros and all starters were fitted with a heat shield (PN 3954224).

Big-block cylinder heads fall into two categories: closed chamber or open chamber. The 396 engines were designed with a restricted combustion chamber area (closed chamber). The low-horsepower 396 engines cylinder heads (casting numbers 3931063 and 3964290) had 101-cc combustion chambers with oval ports and 260-cc intake port volumes. In addition, the intake and exhaust valve combination was a modest 2.06/1.77-inch (intake/exhaust) setup.

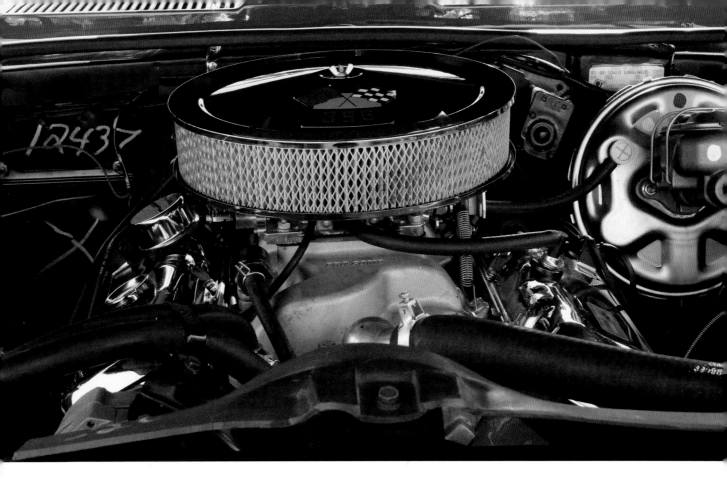

The high-horsepower 396-engine cylinder heads (casting numbers 3919840 and 3964291 for cast-iron versions and number 3919842 for aluminum versions) had 107-cc combustion chambers with rectangular ports and 325-cc intake port volumes. Larger 2.19/1.88-inch valves (Intake/exhaust) were used.

L35 396-CI 325-HP AND L34 396-CI 350-HP

The L34 and L35 engines are almost identical with a couple of exceptions. The 396-ci 325-hp L35 engine was equipped with a cast-iron crankshaft (PN 3874874) whereas the 396-ci 350-hp L34 was fitted with a forged-steel crankshaft (PN 3883944) and a high-lift (.461/.480) hydraulic lifter camshaft.

The L35 engine was fitted with a low-lift (.398/.398) hydraulic lifter camshaft. Both engines were outfitted with cast-aluminum pistons and a 10.25:1 compression ratio. The low-horsepower L35 and L34 396-ci engines used a connecting rod (PN 3933174) with 3/8-inch rod bolts.

A Rochester 4MV Quadrajet 4-barrel carburetor was mounted on a cast-iron intake (PN 3931067) on top of the block. Rochester part number 7016926 was specified for automatic transmission

The L34 and L35 big-block 396-ci V-8 engines are almost identical except for the crankshaft and camshaft. This L35 big-block is rated at 325 hp.

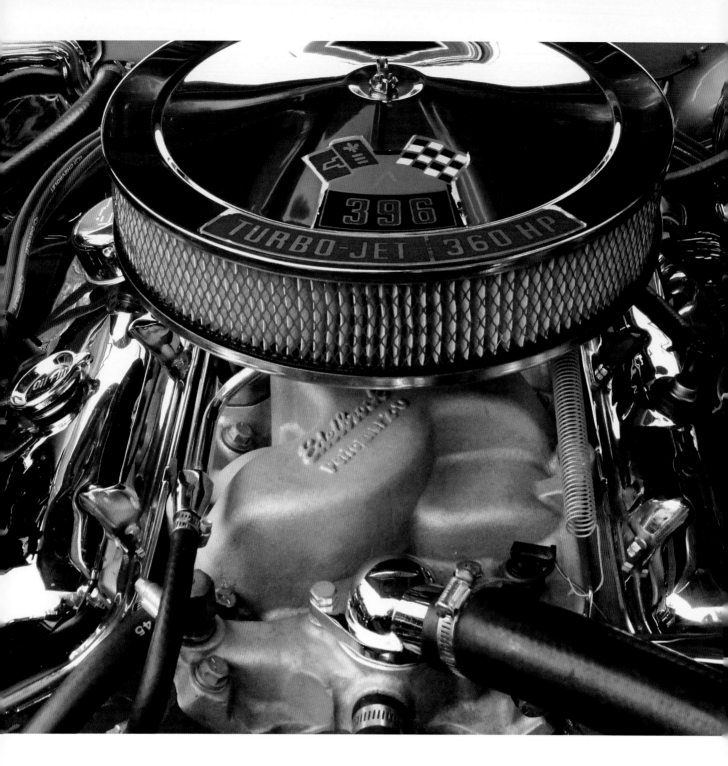

44
1969 Chevrolet Camaro SS
In Detail No. 4

versions and Rochester part number 7016925 was used on manual transmission L35/L34 Camaros.

The cylinder heads used on both the L35 and L34 RPO engines were an oval-port cylinder head with 2.065-inch intake valves and 1.720-inch exhaust valves. The L34 and L35 engines used either the base 37-amp alternator (PN 1100834) for systems without air conditioning or the 61-amp alternator (PN 1100843) with air conditioning.

There were 6,752 L35-equipped Camaros and 2,018 L34 Camaros sold in 1969, which represents 3 percent and 1 percent, respectively.

All Quadrajet-equipped Camaros (350SS, 396-ci 325-hp, and 369-ci 350-hp) were outfitted with an AC fuel filter (GF-432) acting as a supplemental fuel reservoir with a return line to the fuel tank. The high-performance 396- and 427-ci engines with Holley carburetion did not have a supplemental reservoir or return line.

L78 396-CI 375-HP AND L89 396-CI 375-HP

Considered a high-performance big-block, the L78 RPO and L89 engine packages were identical except for the closed-chamber aluminum cylinder heads on the L89. There were 4,889 L78 Camaros sold, 2 percent of the year's total, and only 311 of the aluminum head L89 Camaros sold. These limited-production engine packages had the same 4.094-inch bore and 3.760-inch stroke as the low-performance 396-ci engine packages, but the 11.0:1 compression ratio with forged-aluminum closed-chamber pistons (PN 3878231) helped elevate the L78 and L89 packages. And these high-performance big-blocks

BIG-BLOCK DRIVE PULLEYS

Low-Performance Big-Block (L35/L34)

Description	Part Number
Power steering pulley	3941105 DD
Water pump pulley	3947824 BV or 3947824 DV
Crankshaft pulley	3955291
Harmonic balancer (7-inch)	3860008

High-Performance Big-Block (L78/L89/L72/ZL1)

Description	Part Number
Power steering pulley	3941105 DD
Water pump pulley	3947824 BV or 3947824 DV
Crankshaft pulley	3955291
Harmonic Balancer (8-inch)	3860010

Engine	Block Casting Numbers	Head Casting Numbers
L35 396-ci 325-hp	3931063	3931063
and L34 396-ci 350-hp	3964290	3964290
L78 396-ci 375-hp	3919840	3919840
	3964291	3964291
L89 396-ci 375-hp	3919842	3919842

The L78 and L88 big-blocks are considered high-performance 396 SS engines. Virtually identical, except for the Winters aluminum cylinder heads on the L88 version, these were conservatively rated at 375 hp.

were equipped with an 800-cfm double-pumper Holley 4150 carburetor (PN 3959164GE) bolted to a factory aluminum high-rise manifold (PN 3933163).

The internals were beefed-up to handle the extra horsepower and torque. All high-performance 396- and 427-ci engines had the special tuffrided, forged-steel, cross-drilled crankshaft (PN 3882842). These crankshafts have 2.200-inch journals on the connecting rod pins and 2.749 inches on the main bearing journals. The tuffrided finish and cross-drilling allowed proper lubrication at high RPM. The same solid lifter camshaft (PN 3863143) with high lift (.520 intake, .520 exhaust) was used in the L72 427-ci engine package.

The cylinder heads, both aluminum and cast-iron, had rectangular large ports for improved flow. The cast-iron L78 cylinder heads were fitted with 2.190-inch intake valves and 1.720-inch exhaust valves. All 396- and 427-ci high-performance engines were equipped with GM's heavy-duty connecting rods (PN 3856240). These high-performance connecting rods are referred to as "dimple" rods due to a small dimple cast into the connecting rod near the wrist-pin hole.

L89 ALUMINUM CYLINDER HEADS

The 1969 Camaro L89 aluminum cylinder heads (casting number 3919842)

Winter's foundry handled the casting for the L88 aluminum cylinder heads. These heads can be identified by the iconic "snowflake" logo cast into the sides of the heads.

were nearly identical to the first production big-block aluminum cylinder heads (casting number 3904392), used in 1967 L88/L89 Corvette engines. These aluminum L88/L89 heads were a clone of the cast-iron heads (casting number 3919840) that became the Camaro's L89 aluminum heads. However, a couple of major differences do exist.

The L89 aluminum heads had larger 1.840-inch exhaust valves to move heated exhaust gases quicker. The exhaust manifold mounting flange surface design was changed to prevent gaskets from failing or sliding out when clamping force was applied. The early versions of number 3919842 cylinder heads had two accessory holes drilled and tapped into the end. The later versions had a single accessory hole in each end of the head. Winter's foundry, a long-time GM supplier in Canton, Ohio, handled the casting for these heads. They can be identified by the familiar and iconic "snowflake" logo cast into the components. Unfortunately, Winter's foundry closed in 2000.

DISTRIBUTORS

The Delco-Remy division in Anderson, Indiana, manufactured all distributors in 1969. Those distributors have a model number and date code stamped close to each other. The date code can easily be deciphered.

The first digit is the year. For 1969 the digit is a 9 signifying the last digit of the calendar year.

The next character represents the month of production. The letters A through M represent January through December. The letter I was not used because it could be mistaken for the number 1.

The final digits are the day of the month. For example the date code 9A28 is deciphered as 1969, January 28.

Distributors had color codes applied to the housing, which allowed engine assemblers to identify them without having to read the codes. The GM blueprints call out these color codes. All distributors for the SS model Camaro have an aluminum housing with external adjustment,

OPPOSITE:
Small-block Chevy 350 sleeper engines came equipped with a Rochester 4MV Quadrajet carburetor that offered surprising performance.

DISTRIBUTORS

Engine	Transmission	Part Number	Color
L48 350-ci 295-hp	Manual	1111488	Red or Blue
L48 350-ci 295-hp	Automatic	1111489	Blue
L35 396-ci 325-hp	All	1111497	None
L34 396-ci 350-hp	Manual	1111498	Red
L34 396-ci 350-hp	Automatic	1111499	Purple
L78 396-ci 375-hp	All	1111499	Purple
L89 396-ci 375-hp	All	1111499	Purple

CARBURETORS

Engine	Horsepower	Transmission	Carburetor Model	Part Number
L48 350-ci	295	Automatic	4MV Rochester Quadrajet	7016922
L48 350-ci	295	Manual	4MV Rochester Quadrajet	7016923
L35 396-ci	325	Automatic	4MV Rochester Quadrajet	7029200
L35 396-ci	325	Manual	4MV Rochester Quadrajet	7029201
L34 396-ci	350	Automatic	4MV Rochester Quadrajet	7029204
L34 396-ci	350	Manual	4MV Rochester Quadrajet	7029215
L78 396-ci	375	All	4150 Holley	3959164GE
L89 396-ci	375	All	4150 Holley	3959164GE

a single contact breaker point style with vacuum advance. The high-performance 396 engines with 1111499 distributors feature a long-slot point cam that allows for more timing advance in the distributor.

CARBURETORS

Three companies (Rochester Products, Carter, and Holley) produced carburetors for the 1969 Camaro SS models. The specs always say Quadrajet and Holley, but Carter is known to have built Quadrajet carbs for General Motors throughout the 1960s. "MFG by Carter" cast into the carburetor main body identifies them easily. The specifications and part numbers matched the Rochester components.

Rochester Products Division was acquired by General Motors in 1929, and had been manufacturing carburetors for the automaker since 1932 when the division began specializing in fuel system components. This relationship led to the majority of Camaros in 1969 being outfitted with a Quadrajet carburetor. The medium- and high-performance Camaro engines with Rochester carburetors were 4-barrel versions made at the Lexington Avenue plant in Rochester, New York. Rochester also supplied the low-performance Camaro engine's single- and 2-barrel carburetors from the Bay City, Michigan, plant.

The 350/300, 396/325, and 396/350 engines received the Rochester 4MV Quadrajet 4-barrel carbs. Simple to use and economical, these reliable carbs were rated at 750 CFM that provided decent performance, especially when the larger secondary throttle plates were opened. The third carb supplier, the Holley Carburetor Company, provided the cream-of-the-crop fuel delivery system with the iconic 4150 series carb. Rated at 780 CFM, the modular unit became a favorite with the high-performance enthusiasts and is still very popular today.

OPPOSITE:
This L72 big-block, 1 of 10 1969 Camaros personally tuned and massaged by Dick Harrell, exists in the Classic Industries car collection.

CHAPTER 4

DRIVETRAIN AND CHASSIS

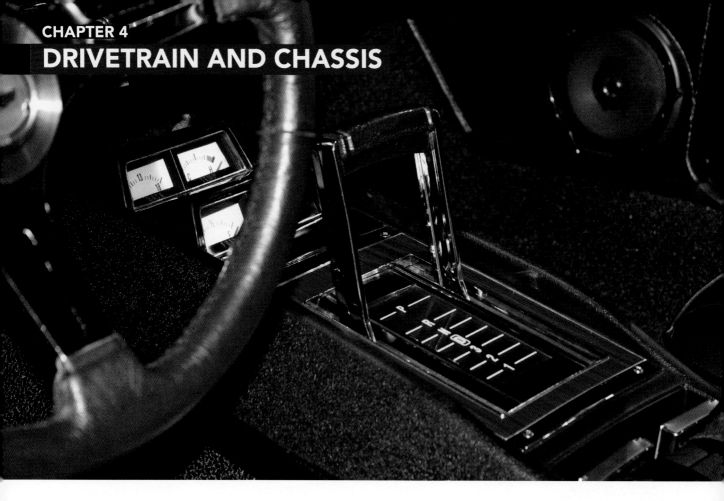

The SS models had an upgraded interior, and this particular car features the horseshoe automatic transmission shifter and full gauge cluster in the console, including water temp, battery voltage, fuel level, and oil pressure meters.

Just as the first-generation Camaros offered a wide range of engine options, the transmission and rear-end options of these cars were just as versatile and equally important to their high-power drivability. Transmissions were available in 3- or 4-speed manual, a 2-speed Powerglide semi-automatic, and two 3-speed automatics.

For high-performance Camaros, rear differentials were the 12-bolt type. Customers were also able to choose a rear axle ratio for their particular driving style and application.

The three-piece-housing rear axle is located in the chassis by a pair of semi-elliptical leaf springs. This traditional semi-elliptical Hotchkiss leaf spring arrangement, which connects the rear axle to the chassis through front and rear shackles and U-bolts, is used in the 1969 Camaro models. Power is transmitted to the rear axle through a traditional driveshaft with two, properly phased, cross-type universal joints. A splined slip shaft connects the driveshaft to the transmission, allowing flexibility and movement between the semi-rigid mounted transmission and the rear axle mounted to the flexible leaf springs.

The Muncie M20 transmission is a highly desirable 4-speed transmission that was optional on all standard and low-performance models. The wide-ratio gears made this gearbox street friendly.

MANUAL TRANSMISSIONS

Transmission options for the 1969 Camaro were virtually the same other first-generation Camaro models. The choices were a 3- or 4-speed manual transmission or a 2- or 3-speed automatic. Different variations were offered with each type.

For example, 3-speed transmission choices included Saginaw or Muncie versions. The same is true for the 4-speed manual transmissions with additional variations in gear ratios. The "close-ratio" gearboxes were offered more for racing applications for which engines ran higher RPM in a narrow powerband. The wide-ratio gearbox was designed for street use, for which engines typically use a broader RPM range.

The 1969 model year saw a federal mandate to provide steering column locks on all new automobiles. In Camaros with manual transmissions, the steering column

MUNCIE MC1 SPECS

1st Gear	2nd Gear	3rd Gear	Casting Number	Extension Housing Casting Number	Side Cover Casting Number
2.42	1.50	1.00	3911940	3911942	3911947

The Muncie M20 was the base 4-speed manual transmission in 1969.

lock mechanism was activated by shifting the transmission into reverse.

3-Speed Manual Transmissions

Three 3-speed manual transmissions were available the 1969 Camaro: a low-performance Saginaw gearbox, the standard-duty Saginaw M15 transmission, and a heavy-duty Muncie MC1 transmission. The focus here is on the high-performance 3-speed. The Muncie MC1 debuted in 1969 and was required when the LM1 engine was ordered. Fully synchronized in the forward gears, the MC1 was side-loaded with the shift lever mechanism on the side, similar to the Saginaw. Built for higher performance, the MC1 had larger bearings, a stronger output shaft and mainshaft, and a larger gearset. The MC1 was included in the SS package for the L48 350-ci small-block V-8, and for L35, L34, L78, and L89 386-ci big-block V-8 engine applications. The SS 350-ci engines required the Muncie MC1 heavy-duty transmission for the optional floor shifter RPO.

4-Speed Manual Transmissions

The base 4-speed manual transmission was assigned the M20 RPO code. As

MUNCIE MANUAL TRANSMISSIONS AND ENGINE COMBINATIONS

Type	1st Gear	2nd Gear	3rd Gear	4th Gear	Engines
Muncie M20 (wide-ratio)	2.52	1.88	1.46	1.00	Z28, LM1, L48, L35, L34, L78, L89
Muncie M21 (close-ratio)	2.20	1.64	1.28	1.00	Z28, L34, 37-hp, 427COPO, ZL1
Muncie M22 (close-ratio)	2.20	1.64	1.28	1.00	Z28, L78, L89, 427COPO, ZL1

with the 3-speed, this gearbox offered a low-performance Saginaw for the L65, LF and L65 small-block 350 V-8 applications.

The Muncie M20 transmission was an option for the high-performance applications, the LM1 and the SS350 small-block V-8s, the SS big-block engines, and the Z28 RPO model. The wide-ratio M20 Muncie was constructed with an aluminum case and offered different gear ratios than the Saginaw M20 4-speed.

A standard performance, close-ratio Muncie was offered for high-performance engine combinations, including the Z28 302-ci L34 big-block, the 427 COPO, and the ZL1 COPO Camaro under the M21 RPO option. A heavy-duty close-ratio Muncie was available for the Z28 and high-performance big-block V-8 engine under RPO M22. The M22 heavy-duty transmission was nicknamed the "Rock-crusher" because of the sound made by the shallow-mesh angle (straight cut) of the gears. The straight angle of the teeth reduced load, stress, and heat, which are important factors when coupled with high-performance engines. In 1969, the M22 Muncie transmission was limited to solid lifter engines, making it the high-performance drivetrain combination.

Manual Transmission Clutch Assemblies

The 3- and 4-speed manual transmissions used a single dry-disc type of clutch with a pressure plate, cover, and drive plate. The pressure plate for 6-cylinder applications was a cast-iron material while those for V-8 applications were stronger nodular-iron plate material. All drive plates were single disc with one friction surface on each side.

Coil springs and flat spring steel between the friction rings provided shock dampening. Standard performance V-8s were equipped with 10.34-inch drive plate friction rings. High-performance V-8 engine applications, such as the SS, received 11.00-inch outside-diameter drive plate friction rings.

Clutch housings for all manual clutch assemblies were manufactured from heavy-duty and lightweight aluminum alloy.

AUTOMATIC TRANSMISSIONS

Four automatic transmissions were used in the 1969 model year: two Power-glide semi-automatic transmissions and two Turbo-Hydramatic (TH) automatic transmissions.

For the first time in 1969, the 3-speed Turbo-Hydramatic 350 (TH350) was offered as a full production-year option as RPO M38 for the 6-cylinder and small-block V-8 engines. The effective Powerglide transmission had reached design limitations requiring General Motors to develop the next level of automatic transmissions for the newer small-block V-8 engines that could benefit from a 3-speed automatic transmission.

The TH350 was beneficial in helping the manufacturer build drivetrains that could pass emissions regulations that were rapidly approaching. Turbo-Hydramatic 400 (TH400) transmissions were classified as heavy-duty transmissions and not efficient for smaller 350-ci and 6-cylinder engines.

AUTOMATIC TRANSMISSION AND ENGINE COMBINATIONS

Type	Drive	Low 2	Low 1	Reverse	Engines
TH350	1:1 direct	1.52:1	2.52:1	1.93:1	L48
TH400	1:1 direct	2.48:1	2.48:1	2.08:1	L35, L34, L78, L89, 427COPO, ZL1

The TH350 transmission's 3-speed gearing was contained in a two-piece assembly consisting of a main housing and an extension housing. The internals consisted of a hydraulic torque converter, planetary gearset, clutch assemblies, and a powerband for friction control. The four clutch assemblies consisted of waved steel with organic-facing drive plates and flat-steel driven plates.

The forward clutch and the direct clutch used four each of the drive plates and driven plates. The intermediate clutch assembly employed two drive and two driven plates, while the low and reverse clutch used four drive and four driven plates.

The torque converter was rated with a stall speed of 2,110 rpm. This cost-efficient M38 TH350 transmission was an option for the 6-cylinder and small-block V-8 engines (L26, L22, LF7, L14, L65, LM1, and L48).

Unlike the TH350, the heavy-duty 3-speed TH400 transmission, sold under RPO M40, had been a production transmission since 1965. The TH400 is fully automatic with a three-element hydraulic torque converter combined with a compound planetary gearset. The internals consist of three multi-disc clutches, a sprag unit, and a roller clutch. Two friction band units control the planetary gearset. The three clutch assemblies consist of waved steel with organic-facing drive plates and flat-steel driven plates. The forward clutch and the direct clutch used five each of drive plates and driven plates. The intermediate clutch assembly employed three drive and three driven plates. The torque converter was also rated with a stall speed of 2,110 rpm.

The TH400 automatic transmission was used successfully in all high-performance Camaros in the 1969 model year (L35, L34, L78, L89, 427COPO, ZL1).

SHIFTERS

The shift levers for manual and automatic transmissions were the remote type, steering-column or floor mounted. All 3-speed manual Camaro transmissions used Muncie shifters in 1969. The 4-speed manual transmissions, either Saginaw or Muncie, used factory-installed Hurst shifters. These manual transmissions used external shift rods to connect to the shift arms projecting from the transmission's side cover as part of the linkage.

The Saginaw 4-speed transmissions called for different shift rods than the Muncie 4-speed. Likewise, the Muncie

The famous horseshoe remote shifter was for automatic transmissions.

The Deluxe three-spoke steering wheel takes center stage and the driver had a clear view of the Deluxe gauge cluster with speedometer, tachometer, and center-mounted clock. This car is equipped with a Muncie 4-speed, and the console-mounted shifter had a plain chrome shifter knob.

The rugged and reliable Chevy 12-bolt limited-slip differential was either the desired option or standard equipment on a variety of Camaros. As the best rear differential offered by Chevy, it features a carrier and pinion support that are integrated into the housing for excellent support and performance.

small-block rod linkage was different that the Muncie big-block rods. The linkage rods connected to either a console-mounted (RPO D55) or a floor-mounted (RPO M11) shifter.

The console-mounted shifter was a plain chrome ball with no additional markings. The floor-mounted shifter was a two-piece ball with the top portion in black with the shift pattern printed top in white. The bottom part of the ball was chrome with a 3/8-inch-diameter thread-locking ring to secure the knob to the shifter.

Camaro models with the TH350 or TH400 automatic transmission were equipped with a column-mounted shift lever unless the chrome "horseshoe" console-mounted shifter was requested. Consoles with floor shifters were popular because many customers saw the Camaro as being less sporty without a

center console. The same console was used with manual and automatic transmissions with the appropriate linkage and shift mechanisms installed. When the RPO U17 option was selected, a special cluster of auxiliary gauges were fitted at the front of the console near the instrument panel. These gauges were mounted in a side-by-side, two-tier design. The console also included a storage compartment, rear-seat ashtray, and courtesy light.

DRIVESHAFT

The Camaro's driveline consisted of a single, tubular, steel driveshaft with two cross-type universal joints in relation to each other on the driveshaft for dynamic balance. The universal joints have pre-packed, anti-friction needle bearings that allow for any temporary misalignment conditions.

The outside diameter of the driveshaft measures 2.75 inches with a wall thickness of 0.065 inch. From the centerline of one universal joint to the other, the length of the driveshaft measures 49.96 inches for all models except those with the L35 engine option. The L35-equipped Camaros with 3- or 4-speed manual transmissions required a driveshaft length of 50.46 inches, also measured from centerline to centerline.

REAR AXLE

GM's 10-bolt and 12-bolt Salisbury-style rear ends were used with all 1969 models. Both rear ends were a three-piece housing design that comprised a cast-iron differential carrier and housing with two steel tubes pressed and welded in. The Salisbury-style differential has a removable cover on the back of the axle housing rather than a removable center section. This allows the carrier bearings to be placed in the axle housing for support. The differential carrier contained a hypoid overhung pinion and ring gear with the drive pinion supported by two tapered roller bearings. The forged and hardened steel axle shafts were designed with an integral drive flange.

The semi-floating axle shafts were supported by axle bearings that were pressed into the axle tube with the outside diameter of the axle shaft acting as the inner bearing brace. These axle bearings were a single row of cylindrical bearings, steel encased, and backed with a spring-loaded seal that was manufactured from synthetic rubber. The drive flanges

were set up with five stud-style wheel retainers with five 7/16-20 UNF-thread hex nuts. The flange studs were arranged in a 4.75-inch circular pattern. The axle shafts were held in place by C-clips inserted over the ends of the axle.

The 10-bolt rear end is often referred to as the "10-bolt" because that's what holds the rear cover in place. The fact that there are also 10 bolts securing the ring gear to the carrier is just a coincidence. Likewise, the 12-bolt rear end has 12 bolts holding the rear cover in place. Both rear ends have a drive pinion vertical offset of 1.50 inches and are adjustable with premeasured shims. In addition to the leaf spring mounts, the rear-end housing had mountings for staggered shocks with the passenger-side shock in front of the axle tube and the driver-side shock located behind the axle tube.

The 10-bolt rear-end ring-gear diameter measured 8.20 inches with a 1.438-inch-diameter pinion gear. The larger 12-bolt ring gear measured 8.875 inches with a 1.625-inch pinion gear. The axle shaft lengths are the same for both sides on both rear ends with the 10-bolt's 28-spline axle shafts measuring 29$\frac{33}{64}$ inches. The 12-bolt axle shafts were 30-spline units measuring 29$\frac{9}{16}$ inches. Both rear ends have the same overall dimensions; they measure 54$\frac{1}{4}$ inches from axle tube flange to axle tube flange, and 42$\frac{7}{16}$ inches between the centerlines of the spring seats.

The 12-bolt rear ends were installed on all SS350s with manual transmissions and Turbo-Hydramatic automatic transmissions (except Powerglide). All SS396 and Z/28 models were also equipped with 12-bolt rear ends. Many 1969 Camaros with the LM1 optional engine received the 12-bolt rear end although a few LM1 Camaros mated with the smaller 10-bolt rear end.

Camaros that were ordered with the factory four-wheel disc brake option were required to have the 12-bolt rear end.

Standard rear-end ratios for the 6-cylinder and 327 V-8 applications with

IDENTIFYING THE REAR AXLE ASSEMBLY

The most practical way to identify your rear axle assembly is to find the axle assembly code. This set of numbers was hand stamped into the passenger-side axle tube at the factory. Although these numbers can be stamped anywhere on the axle tube, they are generally located at the top, facing the front. It is recommended to clean the area thoroughly because the stamped numbers are often weathered with rust, dirt, and road grime.

The seven-digit axle assembly code is divided into several parts that provide the details of the assembly. The first two letters identify the gear ratio (see the chart in "Rear Axle Codes"). The next two digits specify the month when the assembly was made, and the following two numbers provide the day of the month the component was assembled. There is probably another letter followed by a number to identify the plant and shift of the unit's assembly.

MONTH CODE

01	January	05	May	09	September
02	February	06	June	10	October
03	March	07	July	11	November
04	April	08	August	12	December

ASSEMBLY DAY

01 – 31 1st to 31st

ASSEMBLY PLANT

B Buffalo, New York
G Detroit, Michigan
W Warren, Michigan

manual transmissions and Rally Sport with Powerglide were 3.08 and 2.735 for the base Powerglide. For 350 V-8s, the standard ratio was 3.31. For big-block applications, the standard ratio was 3.07 for the manual transmissions and Rally Sport with Turbo-Hydramatic automatic transmissions. The standard ratio for big-block engine applications in the base model was 2.73.

REAR AXLE ASSEMBLIES

Part Number	Application
3961340	12-bolt (JL8 brake option)
3981670	10-bolt (low performance with monoleaf)
3981672	12-bolt (except models with the JL8 brake option)
3981900	10-bolt (medium performance with multi-leaf)

REAR AXLE CODES

Code	Ratio (:1)	Code	Ratio (:1)
BA	2.56	PD	2.73
BB	2.56 Posi	PE	3.08 Posi
BC	3.36	PF	2.73 Posi
BD	3.36 Posi	PG	3.08
BE	4.1	PH HD Posi COPO	3.55
BI	2.73	PK	3.55
BL	3.07	PN	3.08 Posi
BM	3.31	PP	3.36
BN	3.55	PS	3.36 Posi
BO	3.73	PX	2.73 Posi
BP	2.73	PY	2.56
BQ	2.73 Posi	PZ	2.56 Posi
BR	3.07 Posi	QS	2.56 Posi
BS	3.31 Posi	QT	2.73 Posi
BT	3.55 Posi	QU	3.07 Posi
BU	3.73 Posi	QV	3.31 Posi
BV	4.10 Posi	QW	3.55 Posi
BW	4.56 Posi	QX	3.73 Posi
BX	4.88 Posi	QY	4.10 Posi
PA	3.08	QZ	4.56 Posi
PB	2.56	QN	4.88 Posi
PC	2.56 Posi		

*Posi-Traction was required for 3.73:1 and 4.10:1 but optional for other ratios.

COIL AND LEAF SPRINGS

All Camaro models with 6-cylinder engines were fitted with monoleaf springs. Camaro models with engines of 350 ci and larger were fitted with multi-leaf springs with either the 10- or 12-bolt rear end. The Z/28 models used four-leaf springs in contrast to the typical five-leaf multi-leaf springs used in other models.

Spring selection was made at the factory with computer assistance to determine the correct spring based on options and weight listed on the dealer order form. This system was new in 1969 and allowed the factory to "fine-tune" the front and rear springs. Springs wore an identification tag with code letters that identified the rate of the spring. The weight of the vehicle, along with options or deletions, was calculated and the proper spring rate was determined. These letter codes were used to determine the part number of the spring.

According to the GM factory service manual, 23 front coil springs and 18 leaf spring options were used in the computer-aided selection process. "YF" springs were used on base models with no options, or options weighing less than 68 pounds. Cars with options that added weight of 69 to 148 pounds were fitted with "EY" springs. Options that added more than 148 pounds were fitted with "YH" springs.

All big-block Camaro models fitted with the heavy-duty suspension were outfitted with "BK" (PN 3955740) or "BM" (PN 3934894) multi-leaf springs in the rear

Like many other muscle cars, the Camaro had a solid axle, leaf spring suspension, and rear drum brakes.

The rear-axle ratio designation was stamped on the passenger-side axle tube. The two-letter code was part of a larger seven-digit code that provided additional information such as the date of manufacture, the producing plant, and the work shift that made the assembly. Only two variants of the 12-bolt rear axle were offered. The JL8 brake option required shorter axles for the disc brake fitment. General Motors records show only 206 cars were produced with this option, due to the high cost of the upgrade and the short period of availability. At slightly more than $500 for the option, most chose the standard factory brakes.

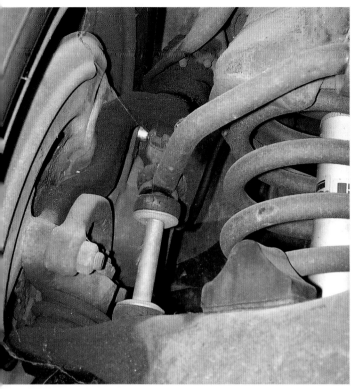

The front coil springs were mounted in the spring bucket of the lower A-arm and another spring mount is found in the chassis. Coil springs have different ratings and were identified by two code letters on a tag attached to the spring.

and "HW" (PN 3955728) and "HQ" (PN 3955724) coil springs in the front.

BRAKES

The standard base brake system for the Camaro was a four-wheel drum-brake system with a Delco Moraine master cylinder designed with dual chambers to prevent total fluid loss. The dual chamber allowed the channel with fluid to work properly, giving the driver the ability to stop in an emergency. Drum-brake cars were fitted with the 5452310 casting Delco Moraine master cylinder except those with power assist, which were fitted with the 5460465 casting number master cylinder. Disc-brake cars used the 5468309 casting number master cylinder.

Power-assisted brakes were a common option with more than 82,890 installed at the factory during the year. The vacuum-operated power assist required less pressure on the brake pedal to stop the car.

As with all first-generation Camaro models, Delco Moraine brake boosters were used on all models. Brake Booster Code 3972 was used on drum-brake vehicles and disc-brake cars received a booster with the Code 9204. This code is stamped on the top of the booster unit.

A twin-compartment master brake cylinder allowed one channel to continue to operate if the other experienced fluid loss.

This brake master cylinder has a vacuum-operated power assist attached to the unit. The power assist required less force on the brake pedal to actuate the brakes.

Front disc brakes, such as these removed from a 1969 Camaro SS, became popular when car owners began to understand the braking power of disc brakes versus four-wheel drum brakes.

Another brake option common on the first-generation Camaro was disc brakes on the front wheels (RPO J52, which included power assist). By 1969, drivers were aware of the improved stopping power of disc brakes. More than three times the number of front disc brakes were installed at the factory in 1969 compared to the previous year, which shows the buyers' understanding of the disc brakes' braking ability, especially in poor weather and wet conditions. As good as disc brakes were, and regardless of the drivers' knowledge of the braking ability of disc brakes, very few cars were ordered with the JL8 factory-installed four-wheel disc-brake option. The Camaro's first factory four-wheel disc brake option was available in 1969, but only 201 were sold. This is one of the rarest options for the entire year and among the rarest of the entire first generation of Camaros.

The J52 disc caliper option consisted of a single-piston floating-caliper design common on most disc-brake cars during that period. This simple design was easy to service and maintain, making it a user-friendly option. The JL8 system used a complex four-piston fixed caliper on all four wheels. Drum brake systems were commonplace and offered few problems for owners.

CHAPTER 5

INTERIOR

The upgraded interior featured a console shifter, wood-grain applique, and full complement of gauges.

Chevrolet's approach to the Camaro earned the coupe a reputation as a lot of car for the money. Performance took shape in many forms, from the wide range of engine options to the generous appointments on the inside. In an era when bucket seats were considered a performance upgrade, the Camaro provided them as stock equipment in 1969. Although the base interior was better than in most passenger cars, plenty of upgrade options could be added. From performance instruments to brightwork or radio options, several trim level options and upgrades were available to personalize the interior for each customer. From the base interior to the custom or special interiors, owners could pick the look and feel that they wanted.

Advertising material from 1969 touted some of the new features for the model such as improved Astro Ventilation system, new bucket seat interior styling with new instrument panel, new interior trim, keyless locking of both doors, and a new steering wheel. Also featured prominently in sales material were the front-seat head restraints, a larger (10-inch) rearview mirror, and, although not new, a foot-operated emergency brake. Of all the design changes made in 1969, the shape of the gauges was one of the most noticeable. The instruments' square appearance in the center instrument cluster was a departure from the standard round gauges in most vehicles.

STANDARD INTERIOR

The Camaro's base interior was well appointed with the Prismatic 10-inch rearview mirror with padded edges, held in place by a satin-finished rearview

The standard interior's instrument panel and dash received features uncommon in most other vehicles' base models. The aftermarket tachometer is mounted on the column.

Passenger compartment doors and quarter panels were trimmed in vinyl with padded armrests. The vinyl-covered headrest is on the passenger's seat.

The RPO D33 passenger-side outside remote-control mirror option was ordered 7,771 times in 1969. The cost was a hefty $11 on the sticker price.

it was actuated by driver- and passenger-door jamb switches. The roof and pillar areas were dressed up with bright roof rail storage clips and trim-colored shoulder belt anchor covers.

The base interior used vinyl on the front bucket seats and the rear bench seat. The front seats were equipped with bright seat adjuster handles and bright front seat-back rest latches. Vinyl front seat head-rests accompanied the bucket seats as mandated by the National Highway Traffic Safety Administration (NHTSA). The headrests were molded poly-urethane foam, in vinyl to match the seat covers, and attached to a chrome bar inserted into the seat back. Because the head restraint law didn't go into effect until January 1, 1969, cars assembled prior to that date were allowed a customer-ordered headrest delete (RPO AR1), a cover over the headrest mounting hardware.

mirror support dressed up with a trim-colored support cover. On either side of the rearview mirror were padded sunshades and padded, trim-colored windshield pillars. Toward the middle of the car, a pair of plastic, trim-colored coat hooks were installed. A standard center dome light with bright bezel occupied the center of the roof in the headliner;

The passenger compart-ment floor was covered with deep-twist carpet and the luggage compartment was finished with splatter paint. Passenger front doors and quarter panels were trimmed in vinyl with padded armrests. A Camaro nameplate and silver-accented, clear plastic window knobs with bright door lock buttons highlighted the door trim. The rear passengers

The RPO Z87 Custom Interior included wood-grain accents on instrument panel and steering wheel, bright pedal trim, and a glove compartment light.

Only 683 RPO N34 Sport-styled steering wheels were ordered from the factory in 1969.

OPPOSITE TOP:
These shoulder belts
are in an Indy pace car
replica. They are typical
of all convertible models.

received an armrest with an ashtray on the rear quarter panel.

The standard interior's instrument panel and dash were treated to uncommon base model features. From the trim-colored instrument panel to the Camaro nameplate on the passenger's side of the dash, the interior was upscale for a personal coupe class. Astro Ventilation outlets on both sides and an Astro Ventilation nameplate is a perfect example of that.

Dash panel controls included a blended air heater and defrost system with lighted controls, bright cowl vent control knobs, a bright black-accented light-switch knob, and dual-speed electric windshield wiper controls with windshield washer. An ashtray with cigarette lighter was a standard feature from another era. Other standard features included front passenger courtesy lights and a glove compartment lock. Standard instrumentation included coolant temperature, generator, and oil pressure gauges; brake warning lights; and high beam and turn signal indicators. A molded-in clock cover with bright Camaro nameplate completed the instrument panel.

The steering column housed the ignition switch with an integral steering wheel and transmission lock. The standard steering wheel was a shrouded two-spoke plastic oval with horn blowing tabs and a bow tie emblem. The left side of the column held a turn signal lever with trim-colored knob. If equipped with a column shift lever, that lever was on the right with a trim-colored knob. A bright hazard flasher knob was also mounted on the column.

IRVING AIR CHUTE COMPANY

Founded in 1919 by Leslie Irvin in Buffalo, New York, the company initially made static-line parachutes. Originally called the Irving Air Chute Company Inc., it was the world's first parachute designer and manufacturer. The company maintains that the company name was inadvertently changed from Irvin to Irving by a secretary that mistakenly added the "g" at the end of the founder's name. Leslie Irvin died on October 9, 1966, but the company continued making safety products through 1969 under the name Irving Air Chute Company. The mistake was finally corrected and the name formally changed to Irvin Air Chute in 1970.

Irving Air Chute manufactured the standard belts for the first-generation Camaro. Interestingly, Irving was the only company to make the standard lap belts for the Camaro. General Motors and Chevrolet used other companies, most notably the Jim Robbins Seatbelt Company and General Safety Corporation to manufacture belts for the other GM and Chevrolet models.

Irvin Automotive Products Inc. continues to make automotive products, including airbags and seat trim, for commercial and mass transportation applications as part of the Takata Corporation.

SEAT BELTS

The Camaro was rated as a five-passenger vehicle with lap belts standard for all passengers, as required by Federal Motor Vehicle Safety Standards (FMVSS). Lap belts were available in two styles: standard and deluxe. The standard version was installed on all interiors unless the deluxe belt option was requested by the customer. Irving Industries made the standard belts, and the deluxe belts were made by Hamill Manufacturing in Washington, Michigan. Both were constructed with 3-panel webbing that was common on the earlier Corvettes.

The standard lap belts had matching plastic covers on the belt and buckle, with the GM emblem on the buckle's push button. The deluxe belts had brushed steel on the buckle. All front-seat belt retractors had plastic covers marked with an "L" (for left side) or "R" (for right side) Colors were chosen at the factory to either match or complement the interior.

Shoulder belts in the coupes were stored on the headliner with clips.

SEAT BELTS

Seat Belt Color Color	Interior Trim Standard	Seat Belt Color Deluxe
Black	Black	Black
Blue	Blue	Blue
Red	Black	Red
Medium Green	Light Green	Light Green
Dark Green	Black	Green
Ivory	Black	Black
Hound's-Tooth		
Orange/Yellow	Black	Black

1969 SEAT BELT MODEL NUMBERS

Belt Type	Standard	Deluxe
Front, lap	2904	1907
Front, shoulder	2950	1952 Coupe/1962 Convertible
Rear, lap	2910	1912 or 1914

Deluxe front and rear lap belts for convertibles were ordered as RPO A39.

Deluxe front shoulder belts for convertibles were ordered as RPO A85.

Deluxe lap belts and front shoulder belts for coupes were ordered as RPO ZK3.

Although lap belts were standard, front shoulder belts were required on all coupes, but optional on convertibles. Rear shoulder belts were an option in 1969, but few were ordered, making this a rare option. Records show only 78 standard rear seat shoulder harnesses (RPO AS5) ordered and 37 deluxe rear seat shoulder harnesses (RPO AS4) installed. The shoulder belt was held on the headliner by belt clips when not in use and mounted inside a plastic routing boot on the floor, on top of the lap belt mount.

The floor anchors had a slight bend in the mounts requiring the belts to be cocked in slightly different angles when being assembled. These model seat belts had an identification tag from the manufacturer containing relevant information such as manufacturer, year, part number (model number), and date code. These tags were not visible by users during normal use or storage.

Convertible shoulder belts were stored with a special clip behind the front seats, near the rear seat armrests.

Standard lap belts had a plastic buckle cover that matched the belt cover, with a GM emblem on the pushbutton.

CUSTOM INTERIOR

The upgraded interior option could be ordered under the Z87 RPO code from dealers. It featured deluxe vinyl or cloth seat trim with molded door panels, dash assist handle, bright pedal trim, and a glove compartment light. Wood-grain accents were added to the shrouding of the base steering wheel, along with wood-grain accents on both driver's and passenger's side dash molding and instrument panel. This enhanced the upgrade look inside the cabin area. The wood grain on the passenger-side dash included the ashtray door and the glove box door. Although not as visible as the trim upgrades, additional body insulation and full molded hood insulation were

added, along with a molded trunk mat to complete the deluxe package.

SPECIAL INTERIOR

Between the standard and deluxe interior packages was a special interior ordered as RPO Z23. Previously set up to be an additional luxury option, in 1969 the Z23 interior features were included in the RPO Z87 package. This package had several of the deluxe interior's visual trim features without the environmental upgrades such as additional insulation in the body and hood. The wood-grain trim on the instrument panel included different radio, windshield wiper, and light switch trim plates. Instrument panel trim molding and dash assist handle were added to the wood-grain steering

wheel shroud as visual enhancements, capped off with bright pedal pad trim.

OTHER INTERIOR OPTIONS WITH SPECIAL RPO PACKAGES

Customers ordering the Rally Sport (RS) package received a black-shroud steering wheel with horn buttons, wood-grain steering wheel treatment, and an RA emblem. The Super Sport (SS) package included the same steering wheel with an SS emblem. Customers ordering the D55 RPO received wood-grain trim on the instrument panel of the console. This option was in a significant number of factory 1969 Camaros. An auxiliary lighting group (RPO ZJ9) combined luggage compartment light

RPO (U25), underhood light (U26), glove box light (U27), front ashtray light (U28), and underdash courtesy lights (U29).

GAUGES AND MONITORING SYSTEMS

The base gauge configuration had a fuel gauge next to the speedometer. If the optional tachometer was ordered without console gauges, the dash was cut out around the Camaro emblem in the center to make room for the fuel gauge. When the D55 RPO console was ordered with the option U17 RPO, the fuel gauge was incorporated into the console. The U17 option could be ordered on V-8 Camaros, but the D55 console was required in order to mount the amp, temperature, fuel, and

High-performance dealer-prepped cars, such as those by Harrell and Yenko, were often treated with enhanced interiors.

A special gauge option (RPO U17 RPO) incorporated the fuel gauge into the floor console.

COPO L72 Camaros typically received Stewart Warner tachometers, which were installed by the dealership prepping the car. This is a Dick Harrell–prepared COPO Camaro.

TACHOMETERS

Description	Part Number	Engine/Availability
7,000 rpm 5,000 redline	6469381	SS350
7,500 rpm 5,500 redline	6469382	396-ci 325-hp, 396-ci 350
7,000 rpm 6,000 redline	6469383	396-ci solid-lifter big-blocks and 427-ci engines

oil pressure gauges. Different underdash wiring harness were used for the special gauge cluster, as well as different wiring and connectors for the tachometer.

Tachometers were offered in three variations. A 5,500-rpm redline, 7,500-rpm maximum tachometer was used on the SS-350 and the 396-ci 325-hp and 350-hp cars. Tachometers with 6,000-rpm redline and 8,000-rpm maximum were originally installed on 396-ci 375-hp big-blocks (January to October). A console was not required with the addition of the tachometer with a center-mounted fuel gauge.

SPEEDOMETERS

The SS Camaro base speedometer had a 120 mph maximum. These speedometers were graduated in units of 10 on the dial face with ticking between the digits. Larger tick marks were placed every 5 mph for quick reference and ease of reading. The rare Speed Warning Indicator option (RPO U15) came with two pointers. The second pointer was an adjustable limit warning indicator that buzzed when the measuring needle reached the limit indicator. Standard speedometers could not be used with the Speed Warning Indicator.

At the base of the speedometer and fuel gauge, and tachometer, if so equipped, were a series of warning indicator lights. The speedometer bezel supported the left turn signal, low-fuel warning, and emergency brake warning lights. The right-hand side held the fuel gauge (tachometer, if fitted), generator, engine coolant temperature, high-beam headlight warning indicator, and right-turn signal warning lights.

OTHER INSTRUMENTS

The Camaro's electric clock was optioned individually with RPO code U35 or as part of the U17 special instrumentation package. The Light Monitoring System (RPO U46) was a rare option and few factory-installed systems exist today. The system was a fiber-optic cable kit that

The electric clock could be ordered separately or as part of the special instrumentation package.

TRIM COLOR OPTIONS

Code	Color
711	Black standard
712	Black custom
713	Black hound's-tooth
714	Yellow hound's-tooth
715	Blue standard
716	Blue custom
718	Red standard
719	Red custom
720	Orange hound's-tooth
721	Medium green standard
722	Medium green custom
723	Midnight green standard
725	Midnight green custom
727	Ivory standard
729	Ivory hound's-tooth
A	White convertible top
B	Black convertible top

Hound's-tooth was not available for convertibles except for the PRO Z11 Indy pace car and replicas. Orange hound's-tooth interior was only available with a Hugger Orange exterior and the yellow hound's-tooth interior was only available with a Daytona yellow exterior.

showed the driver if a light was out. The fiber-optic cable ran from the light housing to the fender bezels in the front and a rear deck monitor in the back. Light shone through the fiber-optic cables when the lights were on and working correctly.

FEATURES AND INDIVIDUAL OPTIONS

The steering column was revised to allow the ignition switch to be moved there from the dash. The change was also made to the optional Comfortilt tilt steering column (RPO N33), for owners looking for a little more comfort and luxury. The tilt columns were black from the factory and were only available for floor-mounted transmission cars.

The base model steering wheel received a redesign in 1969 as well. Previous first-generation steering wheels had three spokes while the 1969 steering wheel had two spokes, and had more in common with GM full-size cars than sports coupes.

The wheel was constructed with a plastic shroud color matched to the interior. The wheel had a rectangular horn button on each spoke. Standard interior cars had a wheel with color-matched shroud and the bow tie emblem. Cars with the Z23 special interior and Z87 custom interior received the wood-grain accent with an emblem in the center depending on the package chosen. An RS emblem was fitted on cars with the Z22 Rally Sport option and an SS emblem was fitted on cars with the Super Sport option. When an SS was also equipped with the RS package, the SS emblem stayed on the wheel center.

Another upgrade (RPO N34) was offered during this model year. A simulated wood-grain, shallow-dish, plastic two-spoke steering wheel with a brushed center hub and bow tie emblem was available at a modest price (about $35). Records show that 6,883 were installed for the year. Simulated walnut grain was used early in production but changed to rosewood grain to match the dash instrument trim after a

The SS was equipped with a 396, which came in four iterations: L34, L35, L78, and L89. This particular SS carries the RS package that includes fender stripes, black-painted grille, and hidden headlights.

wires, and hoses. Different heater and air controls were installed along with different kick panels and air venting to allow the system to work correctly.

Air conditioning was also a popular option with 44,737 factory-installed units sold. The rear window defroster (RPO C50) was far less desirable to buyers, with fewer than 8,000 sold.

Twin front and rear floor mats (RPO B37) were among the most popular options added by buyers for this year's models. Constructed with material similar to the deep-twist floor carpeting, and color-coded to match, this was a bargain option. A folding rear seat (RPO A67) and vanity mirror (RPO D34) were modestly priced but requested far less frequently.

RADIOS

As people began spending more time in their cars, radios became an important accessory. So popular, in fact, that 223,557 factory-installed units were ordered for the model year. Of those, 206,598 were the basic AM pushbutton mono radio (RPO U63) with front tele-scoping antenna.

All AM-FM stereo radios used a solid mast antenna. A bracket held the radio in place securely.

An AM-FM pushbutton stereo radio with a front-mounted fixed-height antenna was the next upgraded option (RPO U69), which cost twice the amount of the base AM radio. At $133.80, the price tag kept the number of sold units down to 8,271.

The Delco AM-FM four-channel stereo pushbutton radio (RPO U79) used in the

The optional simulated wood-grain, shallow-dish, two-spoke plastic steering wheel with a bowtie emblem was a fairly common option.

couple of months. The walnut version of the N34 option is very rare due to the limited run. Manual window crank handles were base equipment on most personal coupes and muscle cars of the era, but electric windows were an option (RPO A31), as was air conditioning. Although we now consider this standard equipment, these were luxury items in 1969.

The Four-Season air conditioning option (RPO C60) required an upgraded 61-amp alternator and heavy-duty radia-tor with a temperature control fan to help control the electrical and engine cooling needs. An entirely different firewall size and shape was used in air-conditioned cars to support the system's evaporator,

1969 Camaro differed from previous GM radios used in previous years; it had a more modern look. Referred to as the "blue light multi-plex" (MPX) stereo radio, the unit's dial and lens had green-tinted numbers, only used in 1969 and 1970 models, with a blue stereo indicator lamp on the radio face. This stereo radio was the only one of this style with a two-piece construction (main unit and amp) and a couple of unique features.

The 1969 radios had a side-mount connector; most other GM radios had connectors on the rear of the case. The Camaro's limited space in the dash created a tight space for mounting the radio so the four-channel AM-FM stereo radio had slanted rear cooling fins to help dissipate heat.

The single-year 8-track tape system with four speakers (RPO U57) was slightly more popular than the U79 "blue light" radio.

Both the multiplex and stereo tape systems had front speakers mounted in the kick panels. The rear package tray speakers were wired down the passenger-side of the car under wiring covers.

INTERIOR SUMMARY

There was no doubt that the 1969 Camaro was the most refined and pleasing to buyers. Clearly, the model redesign was not limited to the exterior, as no stone was left unturned in the interior. From the shape of the instrument cluster to the single-year connector plugs for the radios, the 1969 Camaro was more than just a minor design change. With door-end and tire pressure decals now representing GM's "Mark of Excellence," the engineers had modified almost every part of the Camaro.

The AM-FM pushbutton stereo radio (RPO U69) was one of the most popular radio options.

All AM-FM stereo radios used a solid mast antenna mounted on the front fender.

The Camaro SS Z27 RPO with the 350-ci Turbo Fire engine included brightwork accents and special ornamentation, sport striping, white-letter tires, black-painted body sill, and later in the year, dual exhaust with bright tips.

The beauty of the first-generation Camaro is that the design was simple and similar through the years. Under the sheet metal, the components were almost interchangeable during the first three years. The exterior sheet metal in 1969, however, was a different story. Not only were most of the body panels redesigned, but the trim and brightwork for the 1969 Camaro SS were single-year usage. From emblems to side-marker bezels, many items were unique to the model. This chapter addresses the bits and pieces exclusive to the final year of the first-generation Camaro SS.

PAINT

Camaros were popular for their seemingly endless choices of paint options. In addition to the basic paint configuration, a vinyl top and a convertible top were available options. A new two-tone paint configuration and four

Camaro paint choices ranged from Dover White to Daytona Yellow with black rally stripes as shown here.

striping options, including the iconic Z/28 striping, were available. With the addition of the Pace Car and special paint option, 10 exterior paint options were available that year. The painting process used by General Motors during assembly of the Camaro was the same 11-step process that was standard for Chevrolet.

Essentially, the body was rust-proofed and etched to ensure good paint adhesion. Body and sheet-metal primers were hand sprayed in certain areas to prevent rust. A full primer coat was added to the inside and outside of body panels, followed by flash-primer and primer-surface coats. Initial sanding, including power sanding and hand sanding, were done before three coats of lacquer were applied to the body panels. Next, the body was baked, final sanded, and then baked again to ensure a hard coat of paint with high luster. Undercoating was added during the final stages of assembly. The last step was to fix mars, nicks, or scratches that occurred during

EXTERIOR PAINT CONFIGURATIONS

Basic paint
Basic paint with vinyl top (coupe)
Basic paint with convertible top
    (convertible)
Two-tone paint (coupe only, vinyl top
    not available)
Stripe option DX1
Stripe option D90
Stripe option D96
Pace Car and Z/28 striping
Z/28 with stripe delete
Special paint (included several paint
    schemes)

assembly, followed by a wax and polish for paint protection.

GLASS

By 1969, the FMVSS tightened the performance specifications regarding

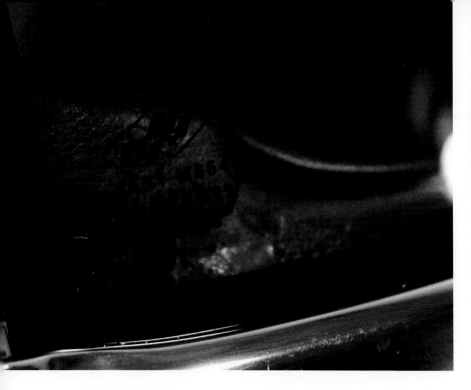

Federal regulations require vehicle glass to have an American Standard and manufacturer model number. This replacement windshield is labeled with AS1, indicating glass that can be used in any location on the vehicle.

TOP RIGHT:
This side-glass window stamp shows that the state required markings "Safety" and "Solid Tempered," along with the manufacturer trade names "Flo-Lite" and "Soft-Ray."

the use of glazing materials (glass) in automobiles. These new standards were enforced on all vehicles manufactured for sale in the United States. General Motors required the glass manufacturers under contract to meet the new requirements. In the Camaro division, General Motors had two primary window and windshield manufacturers in the 1969 model year: Libby Owens Ford (LOF) and Pittsburgh Plate Glass (PPG). LOF supplied glass for most Camaros and PPG supplied it for the Camaro's stable mate, the Pontiac Firebird.

The FMVSS required a standard marking and model number on the vehicle glass during this period. The first required marking, the AS number, was specified by the new standard. AS simply stands for American Standard, with the number following signifying the position where

the glass may be used. During this period, AS1 and AS2 were the two markings used. AS1 indicated the clearest glass, laminated, and suitable for use anywhere in the vehicle but used almost solely in the windshield. AS2 indicated a tempered glass that could be used anywhere except the windshield.

The model number was assigned by the manufacturer. Department of Transportation (DOT) numbers assigned by the NHTSA were also required. In addition to the federal marks, other markings were required by various agencies. It is possible to see the terms "Safety," "Solid Tempered," and "Laminated" etched on the glass because of various state regulations.

General Motors required certain terms on various pieces of glass, including trade names of glass used in the Camaro. "Shaded," "Flo-Lite," and "Soft-Ray"

LIBBEY OWENS FORD GLASS DATE CODES

Here's an example of a Libbey Owens Ford Glass Date Code:

SOFT-RAY
SAFETY L FLO-LITE
AS-2 O AV
F
SOLID TEMPERED

Libby Owens Ford window stamps during this period generally carried a date code on the third line, on the right-hand side. In the example above, the letter A represents September, and the letter V indicates 1969.

MONTH CODE

N January

X February

L March

G April

J May

I June

U July

T August

A September

Y October

C November

V December

YEAR CODE

A 1966

Z 1967

X 1968

V 1969

T 1970

were often added to indicate tinting or type of glass. When tinting was added to windshields, "Shaded" was marked on the windshield. Tinting on other glass was often the blue tinting that General Motors designated with the trade-name "Soft-Ray," which was etched into the glass.

Date codes were added to the glass markings by the manufacturer, with letter codes indicating the month of manufacture.

LAMPS AND MARKERS

The taillamps were changed to fit the newly redesigned Camaro. They were wider with a three-segment construction instead of the previous two segments. These were fashioned in a "saw tooth" design that enhanced the appearance of the rear end. The Rally Sport reverse lamp was different and used a wiring harness unlike other models and the previous year's version. The RS reverse lamps were mounted in the rear valance, below the bumper. The side-marker lights were smaller and more aerodynamic looking with an amber light in front and a red light in the rear.

STANDARD BASE CAMARO EXTERIOR

The fresh body lines created new body panels for the nose, fenders, quarter panels, and tail, which necessitated changes in the grille, body sill molding, and exterior brightwork. The front fenders were appointed with Camaro nameplate emblems. Most were fitted with standard

The taillamp units were changed for the new model year. The wider, three-segment taillamps suited the freshly redesigned exterior.

hubcaps, but six optional hubcaps and trim rings were available for base model Camaros by special order. Side-marker lights were smaller than the previous year and the 1967 Camaro didn't have side-marker lights at all.

RALLY SPORT EXTERIOR

Selecting the Rally Sport option added a distinctive grille with concealed headlights and RS badge on the nose. The Rally Sport headlamp doors were body colored with three sets of slits, to let the headlight shine through if the doors failed to open. Interestingly, the RS's windshield washer reservoir was relocated for 1969 to allow for the vacuum reserve tank for the headlight doors. The front fender emblems were identical to the

base Camaro, but the fender nameplate was an RS badge. The body sill below the doors was painted black with body sill molding. An RS emblem was affixed to the rear panel and the back-up lights were positioned below the rear bumper in the rear cowl. Front parking lamps were installed in the lower valance, below the bumper. Bright taillamp trim rings accompanied the Z22 RPO option. Like the base Camaro, standard hubcaps were typically fitted but six optional hubcaps and trim rings were available by special order.

CAMARO SUPER SPORT EXTERIOR

The SS was easily identified by a black grille with SS badge in the front and a black panel in the rear. If equipped with

a big-block engine, an SS emblem was affixed to rear panel, warning enthusiasts looking for a challenge. The SS received the sport striping (hockey stick) that has become the iconic look for big-engined pony cars.

A special hood with simulated intake ports was one of few horizontal panels changed in 1969, and only on the SS, SS/RS, and COPO models. Front-fender engine emblems with either 350 SS or 396 SS emblems and the SS nameplate were a part of the package, in addition to white-letter wide-oval tires with 14 x 7–inch wheels and eight hubcap and trim ring options.

CAMARO SS/RS EXTERIOR

Upgrading the Super Sport with the Rally Sport package added a black grille with concealed headlights and the SS badge. The hockey stick sport stripes with front fender engine emblems and SS nameplate were also affixed. The black body sill and molding, along with the special hood with simulated intake ports were part of this model. Cars with big-block engines wore a standard SS black rear panel with the SS emblem and back-up lights in the lower cowl, below the rear bumper. Front parking lamps were installed in the lower valance, below the bumper. As with the base Camaro Rally Sport model, bright taillamp trim rings accompanied the Z22 RPO option along with white-letter wide-oval tires, 14 x 7–inch wheels, and eight hubcap and trim ring options.

VINYL AND CONVERTIBLE TOPS

Of the 225,512 Camaro coupes manufactured in 1969, records show that

Camaro Super Sport 396s were offered in the following packages: a base with 325 hp, an engine producing 350 bhp, and the 375-bhp. Chevy bolted aluminum heads to the L78 and thus created an L89 with 375 bhp.

This Camaro SS/RS wears aftermarket wheels. The SS package featured high-performance springs and shocks, F70 x 14 tires, power front disc brakes, and non-functional hood scoop.

The D80 spoiler option was sold in an early version, in the same size as the 1968 spoilers, and a late version, which was wider. The closeup photo shows how much the spoiler extends past the edge of the decklid.

100,602 were fitted with vinyl tops, making it one of the most popular options. With several color options available, buyers could pick any fabric color to go with any body color by ordering through a Chevrolet dealer.

Convertible tops were offered in black, medium blue, and white, with colors suggested to complement a range of body colors. Much as with vinyl tops, customers could custom order any available color combination using a dealer order form. The retractable convertible top was available in a manual or power configuration. The manual configuration was standard for the body style; however, 9,631 of the 17,573 convertibles manufactured in 1969 (almost 55 percent) were ordered with the power option.

SPOILER OPTION

Customers could order an optional spoiler (RPO D80) that included a rear

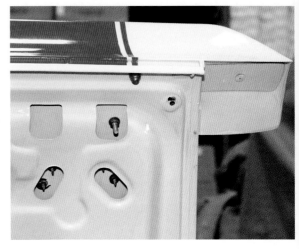

decklid-mounted fiberglass spoiler and plastic front lower valance. Early in the model year, the factory used up the 1968 spoilers when the option was ordered. When the supply ran out, a wider spoiler that was designed to fit the newly redesigned Camaro body was used. These later spoilers stretched across the full width of the Camaro rear end. The early spoiler, although shorter in width, had a steeper angle than the later version. Most Camaro enthusiasts preferred the wider spoiler as its aggressive look complemented the car's wider and lower look.

GRILLE

The 1969 Camaro grille was available in two basic designs: a standard version with exposed headlights and a Rally Sport version with hidden headlights. Both grilles were more angled and "V" shaped than the previous first-generation Camaro models, giving them a stealthier appearance. Headlight surrounds were plastic on standard grilles and the RS models had bright metal rings securing the headlight to the housing. Standard grilles were

argent silver, except for SS models, which were treated to flat-black paint for the famous SS "blacked-out" grille.

EMBLEMS AND BADGING

Standard badging for 1969 Camaro models included a grille emblem, two engine-size fender emblems, two "Camaro" fender emblems, one "Camaro by Chevrolet" header panel emblem, one "Camaro by Chevrolet" trunk lid emblem and a rear panel emblem. These emblems were typically plastic units plated with a chrome-like finish. Engine-size fender emblems were painted white with chrome edges. The 350 fender emblems were installed on the base, RS, SS, and SS/RS models as appropriate. The coveted 396 fender emblem was used on the SS and SS/RS models equipped with 396-ci engines.

SS models also received special fender treatment with two-piece "SS" front fender emblems on the 350- and 396-engine models. The emblems were painted white with a polished outer chrome border. A similar SS emblem was fitted to the grille on 350, 396, and SS/RS models.

The standard grille with exposed headlights was restyled for 1969 and is one of the most distinctive and attractive features on the car.

The Rally Sport has the same center apex as the standard grille, and headlights are tucked away behind vacuum-actuated doors.

CAMARO BODY PAINT CODES

Solid or Bottom Color Code (Two-Tone) and Color Name

10 Tuxedo Black	61 Burnished Brown
40 Butternut Yellow	63 Champagne
50 Dover White	65 Olympic Gold
51 Dusk Blue	67 Burgundy
52 Garnet Red	69 Cortez Silver
53 Glacier Blue	71 LeMans Blue
55 Azure Turquoise	72 Hugger Orange
57 Fathom Green	76 Daytona Yellow
59 Frost Green	79 Rallye Green

Top Body Color Code (Two-Tone) and Color Name

50 Dover White	53 Glacier Blue
51 Dusk Blue	63 Champagne

FACTORY SUGGESTED TWO-TONE COMBINATIONS

Lower Code Color	Upper Code Color
53 Glacier Blue	50 Dover White
55 Azure Turquoise	50 Dover White
53 Glacier Blue	51 Dusk Blue
51 Dusk Blue	53 Glacier Blue
65 Olympic Gold	50 Dover White
61 Burnished Brown	63 Champagne

FACTORY SUGGESTED COLOR COMBINATION

Vinyl Top Code Color

B	Black	All exterior colors
C	Blue	Dover White, Glacier Blue, Dusk Blue, Cortez Silver
E	Parchment	All exterior colors
F	Brown	Olympic Gold, Butternut Yellow, Champagne, Burnished Brown
S	Green	Tuxedo Black, Dover White, Frost Green, Fathom Green

Black and White convertible tops were available with all exterior colors.

The "Camaro by Chevrolet" emblem, designed because Chevrolet was initially worried about name recognition for the new model, was installed on all 1969 Camaro models on the header panel. This emblem was also installed on the trunk lid if a spoiler was factory-installed.

By 1969, the Camaro did not suffer from name recognition, but the emblems were still installed at the factory. A Camaro fender emblem featuring the name in script was installed on the front fenders of all Camaros except the RS. The bowtie grille emblem was installed on all base Camaros but not on the RS or SS. A bowtie rear panel emblem was installed on all Camaro models, including COPO and other high-performance dealer models without RS, Z/28, or SS options.

One of the most iconic trim pieces of the first-generation Camaro, the chrome simulated-vent grilles, were installed on the Rally Sport's quarter panels, over the simulated louvers molded into the quarter panel. These ornaments (PN 3928528) were die-cast and chromed. Equally famous, the SS hood louvers (PN 393930910 passenger's side and PN 393930909 driver's side) were fitted to all Camaro SS models equipped with 350 or 396 engine. The louvers were diecast and chrome plated with black-painted accents. Care was taken to fit the curvature of the hood, helping create a smooth surface on the sheet metal. The recesses were designed with drain holes to prevent the collection of water.

The fender emblem signified that a high-horsepower 350 small-block resided in the engine bay.

The 396 emblem indicated that a Mark IV big-block engine was under the hood.

The 427 engine fender emblem meant that this Camaro SS carried an L72 with iron block and aluminum heads. The ZL-1 was an all-aluminum Can-Am-derived engine at 425 hp. To get the 427 engine option, a customer had to order an SS model and request the special engine upgrade. That makes all COPO and 427 Camaros Super Sport versions.

The "Camaro by Chevrolet" emblem.

The Camaro script-style fender emblem with the two-piece SS emblem.

The Rally Sport's chrome grille covered the simulated side vent louvers.

The SS simulated intake hood louvers became one of the most recognizable ornaments on the SS Camaro.

The stripes painted at the factory on factory-installed spoilers did not go to the end of the decklid.

The factory-painted D90 Sport stripe has a break for the front fender engine emblem.

STRIPING

The first-generation Camaro models represented the first Chevrolet-produced cars with factory-painted stripes. Although the Z/28 models set the stage, the 1969 SS D-90 hockey-stick stripes stole the show. Other 1969 stripe options included the simple D96 stripes and the DX1 option, which was the reversed version of the 1968 L48 stripe.

D90 Sport Stripe

The D90 "hockey stick" stripe was modified for 1969. Instead of crossing the header and running down the fender and the door, the new iteration was only on the fender and the door. This optional stripe was painted from the lower front fender, ascending up the fender where it broke for the engine badging. On V-8 cars, the stripe continued on after the badging, where it made a 90-degree turn toward the tail, continuing to the door.

On cars with the inline-6, the fender stripe was solid because of the absence of a fender emblem. The door stripe was a vinyl tape decal instead of paint. These stripes were available on the base and SS models in black, white, and red. Red was reserved for the burgundy and tuxedo black body paint but could be special ordered on other body colors.

DX1 Stripe

The DX1 stripe was new for 1969, and an uncommon option with fewer than 20,480 ordered. It featured two stripes originating at the header panel and continuing along the centerline of the hood toward the windshield. These stripes were not as popular, and despite only being available on non-SS and non-Z/28 Camaros, they have remained an oddity in Camaro circles. Even though they are rare, this option does not demand a higher price when offered at auction.

D96 Body Side Stripes

The D96 pinstripes over fender wells were even more rare than the DX1 stripes with only 5,176 ordered. Although the individual RPO was not popular, this option was included in the Rally Sport option and the style trim group (RPO Z21). It was also included in the Indy pace car replica models (RPO Z11), which also used the Z/28 stripes. This is the only time that the D96 stripes and Z/28 striping appear together.

The D96 stripe was a pinstripe that started at the front fender at the wheel opening and followed the body line onto the door. The rear quarter panel pinstripe also came from the front of the opening and followed the body line to the end of the body. These stripes were hand painted at the factory.

WHEELS AND TIRES

Three steel wheels were available for the Camaro with 14-inch diameters on all but the Z/28, which wore 15-inch wheels. The wheels were manufactured by the Kelsey-Hayes Company in Michigan, and are stamped with Kelsey-Hayes codes

The Z27 Super Sport RPO option included the Goodyear Polyglas F70 x 14 white-letter tires with 17 x 7–inch wheels.

A space-saving spare replacement for the F70 x 14 tire (RPO N65) was standard for the 1969 Camaro.

WHEEL AND TIRE SPECS

Wheels

Model	Size	Style	Code	Brakes	
Camaro SS	14 x 7	JJ	SS	AO	Disc
Camaro SS/COPO	14 x 7	JJ	Steel	XT	Disc
Camaro SS	14 x 7 JJ	SS	YA	Disc	RPO N66
Camaro SS	14 x 7 JJ	Rally	YJ	Disc	
Optional/Base	14 x 6 JK	Rally	XN	Drum	
With front disc	14 x 6 JJ	Steel	XF	Disc	

Tires

Model	Standard	Optional
All models except SS and Z/28	E78x14	F70x14
SS Models	F70 x 14 white-letter white or red stripe	F70x14

RPO	Description
N65	Space saver spare tire for E78 x 14 blackwall (not for JL8 disc brakes)
	Space saver spare tire for E78 x 14 whitewall
	Space saver spare tire for F70 x 14 red or white stripe
	Space saver spare tire for F70 x 14 white-letter
	Space saver spare tire for F70 x 14 fiberglass-belted
PK8	E78 x 14, 2-ply whitewall tires
PL2	E78 x 14, fiberglass-belt blackwall tires
PL3	E78 x 14, fiberglass-belt whitewall tires
PL4	F70 x 14, fiberglass-belt white-letter tires
PL5	F70 x 14, white-letter tires (Included with the SS Model)
PU6	E70 x 15, white-letter tires (Z/28)
PW7	F70 x 14, white-stripe tires
PW8	F70 x 14, red-stripe tires
PY4	F70 x 14, fiberglass-belt white-stripe tires
PY5	F70 x 14, fiberglass-belt red-stripe tires

near the valvestem hole. They were mostly painted in the body color, unless outfitted with full wheel covers, and then the wheels were painted semi-gloss black. The wheel backs were painted flat black. Rally wheels were painted argent silver.

Dealer-prepped high-performance COPO models, such as the Yenko COPOs, were reported to use Pontiac rally wheels due to the wider design of the spokes. The spokes were painted argent silver with the recessed coves painted semi-gloss black. Goodyear, Firestone, and Uniroyal all supplied tires as standard equipment during the model year. A sports car conversion package was available for COPO Camaros that deleted the standard F70 x 14-inch wheels and tires and replaced them with E70 x 15–inch Goodyear Wide Tread GT tires on 15 x 7–inch rally wheels.

Standard hubcaps and trim rings (RPO P06) were available for all trim levels and models. Also available on the base, RS, and SS models were the full wheel cover (RPO P01), mag style wheel cover (RPO N96), mag spoke wheel cover (PA2), the simulated wire wheel cover (RPO N95), and the Rally Wheel (RPO ZJ7). The Sport wheel cap (RPO N66) was available on the SS models.

TOP LEFT: Standard steel wheel with full wheel cover and incorrect period tire.

TOP RIGHT: Rally wheel with trim ring and incorrect period tire.

BOTTOM LEFT: A reproduction Polyglas RWL F70 x 14 tire. Originals did not have the size in raised white letters.

BOTTOM RIGHT: The highly desirable Yenko sport wheel with center cap.

MUSCLE CARS

IN DETAIL

Each volume in the all-new In Detail series from CarTech provides an incredible amount of detail on a single model of an iconic muscle car, all at a very affordable price. Included is an introduction and historical overview, an explanation of the design and concepts involved in creating the car, a look at marketing and promotion, and an in-depth study of all hardware and available options, as well as an examination of where the car is on the market today. Also included is an appendix of paint and option codes, VIN and build-tag decoders, as well as production numbers

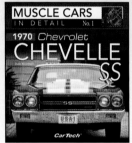

1970 CHEVROLET CHEVELLE SS: In Detail No. 1 *by Dale McIntosh* After the General Motors displacement ban ended for the 1970 model year, Chevrolet put new skin on the Chevelle and a new powerplant under the hood: the vaunted LS6 454 with 450 hp. Today, the 1970 Chevelle SS 454 is viewed as one of the most iconic automobiles ever produced on American soil. SS 396 and 454 Chevelles command a premium at auction and are one of the most coveted muscle cars ever produced. 8.25 x 9", 96 pgs, 110 photos. Sftbd. Part # CT588..***$18.95***

1971 PLYMOUTH 'CUDA: IN DETAIL NO. 2 *by Ola Nilsson* In terms of performance, the 1970-1974 Barracudas and Challengers were every bit the measure of the Ford and GM offerings. By 1971, the handsome Barracuda had established itself as one of the best-performing cars in the marketplace. Ordering the 'Cuda, owners could lay waste to Mustang and Camaro owners with such stout engine packages as the 440-6 and 426 Hemi. No other mass-production Pony Car can consistently claim asking prices of $2,000,000 for its top model in today's prices. 8.25 x 9", 96 pgs, 110 photos. Sftbd. Part # CT576..................***$18.95***

1968 SHELBY MUSTANG GT350, GT500 AND GT500KR: IN DETAIL NO. 3 *by Greg Kolasa* In 1968, Ford sought to take over much of the process of producing Shelby Mustangs and increased the production dramatically to meet anticipated sales demand. In an effort to appeal to muscle car fans rather than race fans, the cars were losing their edgy race car feel and were becoming more high-end performance road cars with a long list of performance and comfort options including 428 Cobra Jet engines, automatic transmissions, and air conditioning. They may have no longer been sports cars, but they were now fantastic muscle cars. 8.25 x 9", 96 pgs, 110 photos. Sftbd. Part # CT572 ....***$18.95***

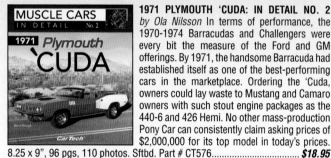

Muscle Cars In Detail #4
1969 Chevrolet Camaro SS
By Robert Kimbrough

Now that you are the proud owner of this book, check out all the other titles in this exciting series.

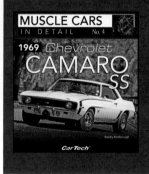

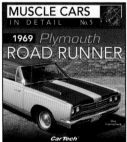

1969 PLYMOUTH ROAD RUNNER: In Detail No. 5 *by Wes Eisenschenk* Volume No. 5 of CarTech's In Detail series covers the 1969 Plymouth Road Runner. It was an interesting marriage of a car that attempted to appeal to potential buyers with a low cost, light weight, and potent bare-bones package. It also added the brilliant marketing strategy of partnering with a famous studio and a popular cartoon character. The end result was a wildly popular, big-block, affordable muscle car with great graphics and a cool beep-beep horn. The public loved it. 8.25 x 9", 96 pgs, 120 photos, Sftbd. Part # CT580 ..... ***$18.95***

1973–1974 PONTIAC TRANS-AM SUPER DUTY 455: In Detail No. 6 *by Barry Klyczyk* Pontiac ushered in the muscle car era when it introduced the mid-size 1964 GTO with a 389. It was fitting that Pontiac made the last legitimate muscle cars of era: the 1973 and 1974 Trans Am Super Duty 455. This book goes behind the scenes to reveal how a cadre of personnel at Pontiac refused to relinquish high-performance, forged ahead, and built the last great muscle car. He covers the design, development, and manufacture of each major component of the group as well as engine development and special equipment of the Super Duty 455 engine. 8.25 x 9", 96 pgs, 110 photos, Sftbd. Part # CT583...........***$18.95***